The Austrian Empire

PROBLEMS IN
EUROPEAN CIVILIZATION

Under the editorial direction of
John Ratté
Amherst College

The Austrian Empire
Abortive Federation?

Edited and with an introduction by

Harold J. Gordon, Jr.
University of Massachusetts

Nancy M. Gordon

D. C. HEATH AND COMPANY
Lexington, Massachusetts   Toronto   London

Burgess
DB
86
.G63
copy 3

Copyright © 1974 by D. C. Heath and Company.

All rights reserved. No part of this publication may be reproduced or transmitted in any form or by any means, electronic or mechanical, including photocopy, recording, or any information storage or retrieval system, without permission in writing from the publisher.

Published simultaneously in Canada.

Printed in the United States of America.

International Standard Book Number: 0-669-90456-2

Library of Congress Catalog Card Number: 73-21185

CONTENTS

III NEW FORCES, INDUSTRIALISM, SOCIALISM, AND WORLD WAR I

IV THE EMPIRE IN RETROSPECT

INTRODUCTION

Americans are accustomed to think of the federal form of government as something peculiarly their own, invented by the founding fathers expressly to accommodate the unique situation of the newly independent colonies in the New World. They forget that federalism has a long, if not much honored, history in the Old World, beginning with the leagues of city-states in the Hellenistic world. These leagues derived their origins from precisely those circumstances which appear always to have led to a search for workable federal institutions, namely, a desire to accommodate unhindered local autonomy and diversity in a larger political system. The larger unit most often sprang from a need to protect local independence from outside aggression and interference.

Practical experience has thus led to a definition of federal government as ". . . any union of component members, where the degree of union between [sic] the members surpasses that of mere alliance, however intimate, and where the degree of independence possessed by each member surpasses anything which can fairly come under the head of merely municipal freedom."[1]

The great difficulty with most federal forms of government has been that of defining the exact spheres of the federal authorities and those of the local governments which make up the federal body. This requirement has generally led in time to a written constitution, which spells out clearly the respective powers of state and federal government; to a judiciary whose task is to interpret this division of federal and local powers in specific cases; and to a legislature which in its

---

[1] E. A. Freeman. *History of Federal Government in Greece and Italy* (New York, 1893), p. 2.

organization recognizes the role played by the more local authority —state or city-state—in the formation and the continued operation of the federal government. We know that the U.S. Senate's equal representation of each state was designed to acknowledge the separate identity of the states within the federal system.

The sense that local needs can best be met by local government is at the heart of the federalist viewpoint. The critical issue is to find the point at which larger necessities can come together with local pressures and local sensitivities, can provide just that degree of union which the common good absolutely requires in a framework allowing as much diversity and individual freedom as possible. The attempt to find this point characterizes the whole of the history of the last seventy years of the Austro-Hungarian Empire and justifies the interest of modern American students, for the inhabitants of the Austro-Hungarian Empire had many problems which are reflected in America. Foremost of these is unquestionably the ethnic diversity of the population, but add to this religious variety, the divergent requirements of industry and agriculture, and the overriding desire on the part of society's leaders to create some sense of unity and common purpose, some feeling of "manifest destiny." The slogan "variety in unity," which Francis Joseph, the next to last emperor, recommended to his subjects, could well be our own.

The history of the attempts to create a federal empire from the Austro-Hungarian monarchy really begins in 1804, when the then monarch, Francis of Habsburg-Lorraine, declared himself emperor of Austria. In so doing he conferred the name Austrian Empire on the dynastic conglomeration of kingdoms, principalities, duchies and provinces he had inherited. Francis thus took the first step in molding out of his varied possessions a modern empire held together by geographic contiguity, shared institutions, and the common interests of its inhabitants. The common interests were then basically self-defense, a desire to remain free of French tributary exactions under their aggressive emperor, Napoleon I. The shared institutions consisted almost exclusively of the person of the monarch; geographic contiguity, assured by the loss of Belgium, focused around the great Danubian plain girdled by the Carpathian Mountains. Thus Austria became essentially the land of the Danube Valley, though it also held fringe areas which did not in any fundamental way belong geographically to the valley.

The focal point in this political structure was the person of the monarch, initially because it was common allegiance to him that gave the Austrian Empire of 1804 a rudimentary unity, ultimately because his desire for the preservation of his realm, and with it his dynasty, formed the principal impetus for constitutional rejuvenation. It was his perennial consciousness of the risks, real or sometimes fancied, to Austrian survival from abroad which led him on the one hand to entertain schemes for governmental revision, on the other to set limits to those schemes. Thus for all that moderns now judge monarchs as wholly passé, even as symbol, let alone as active participant in politics, the then Austrian monarch formed a vital element in the Austrian picture, one whose presence was accepted by virtually all elements of society. (Republicanism was the faith of a minority of Europeans before 1914 and had scarcely any adherents in eastern Europe.)

Yet while the monarch provided the impetus to constitutional change, whether for tactical or strategic reasons, he had to rely on his advisors for the details of those changes. Thus the first great period of constitutional experiment, that of the Schwarzenberg ministry immediately following the Revolution of 1848, is really the story of the two great innovators of that regime. As the emperor relied upon Schwarzenberg, the minister-president, so the minister-president relied upon the two great specialists of his government, Count Francis Stadion and *Freiherr* von Bruck. The one was a specialist in local government, the other in economics. The first devised plans for local government reform, which would give the subjects of Francis Joseph practical political experience. The second proposed a vast scheme whereby the economic conditions of prosperity and its mid-nineteenth-century result, a rapidly expanding middle class, might produce new groups with a vested interest in the status quo, groups who might find in local government and in industry and trade rewarding spheres for themselves.

Yet the vision of Schwarzenberg and his colleagues, whatever its intrinsic merits, never had an opportunity to advance far. Whether this was the result of bad faith on the part of Schwarzenberg and the emperor, of the untimely death of one of the principal innovators, of pressures from abroad, of the lack of resources at home, or perhaps all of these together remains for historical debate. We do know that renewed constitutional advance received fresh impetus from without: the defeat of Austria at the hands of Napoleon and Piedmont-Sardinia in 1859 led to a new search for a broader constitutional structure, embracing more elements of the population.

The decade of the 1860s, between the defeat of 1859 and the defeat of 1866 at the hands of Prussia, is a period of intense constitutional exploration and attempted innovation. That the end result, the Compromise of 1867, provided no more than a modicum of constitutional government in the western half of the empire while it handed the eastern part of the empire wholly over to the tender mercies of the Hungarian aristocracy was a disappointment to all concerned, except perhaps the Hungarian beneficiaries. Yet it too provides an object lesson in politics as the art of the possible.

Even though experimentation with the central constitution of the empire came to an end with the Compromise of 1867—except for the introduction of universal manhood suffrage in the western half in 1907—experimentation with government, new ideas, and new proposals continued to surface after that time. Real progress was made in some areas of Austria toward the alleviation of competing national pressures; new movements—industrialism and socialism—offered new forms, new outlets, for the restless energy of the Austrian peoples. That these were not more successful in satisfying popular desires is not wholly the fault of the protagonists: worldwide forces played an important, perhaps a decisive, role, culminating in the First World War.

Retrospect has won back for the Austrian monarchy some of the prestige it lost in the ignominy of its collapse. For one thing, the history that Utopians among us would gladly forget—because history always mixes the bad with the good—is less easily discarded than these Utopians would like to believe. Even though historic forces may not altogether shape the future, they can set limits to it. In one respect perhaps, the story of the Austrian monarchy is a story of the disastrous neglect of a recognition of those limits. The monarchy's reformers, like parliamentary reformers everywhere in the nineteenth century, sought legitimacy for their claims in the "historic" rights of the various nationalities, forgetting that a recognition of historic right claimed by one nationality entailed acknowledgment of their validity by other, competing national groups. Too often, though the reformers castigated the monarchy for clinging to outmoded historic claims, they set their own claims in opposition to a realistic settlement in which each element would gain something, but none would get everything they desired—and which perhaps "historic right" might seem to justify.

Each succeeding attempt at solution made it clear that it was less the resistance of the monarch to a loss of historic powers than the refusal of each nationality to allow any recognition of the other nationalities' claims, historic or otherwise, which prevented constitutional progress.

Intervening history has since shown that although the monarchy appeared to the nationalities within it as an intolerable straitjacket, removal of that framework did not in fact confer any greater measure of freedom on the ordinary individual living in that area, often quite the contrary. The creation of the network of peoples' democracies under Russia's aegis after World War II offered a kind of ex post facto proof for the main contention of the monarchy's supporters, namely, that the monarchy was a political, as much as an historical, necessity. If the area did not possess its own indigenous empire, it would sooner or later form part of the empire of some neighboring superpower, be it Hitler's Germany or Stalin's Russia.

Finally, retrospect has shown that good government, successful government, is above all that which knows the art of compromise. The ultimate political compromise is a federal form of government in which each participant enjoys some scope for the realization of his aims, yet this freedom is always limited by the spheres rightfully assigned to others. While the monarchy may have suffered in some respects from being forever in a state of noncommitment, or more often commitment in several directions at once, yet it is arguable that a network of constructively competing obligations and responsibilities is the highest form of political union. In the Austrian monarchy this kind of self-restraint was scarcely to be found; yet newer circumstances, above all the risks of a nuclear world, endow federalism with a respectability which justifies studying the Austrian Empire as an object lesson in missed opportunities.

Conflict of Opinion

Considering that here was the heir to a great empire, scarcely grown out of boyhood and until then always shielded from injustice and from the rest of the world, who began his royal career with a lie of which he must have been conscious, one can appreciate the tragedy which fastened itself on the hitherto guiltless Francis Joseph at this moment and never left him. The old poetic prophecy of the "evil deed which must continuously produce new evil" found here appalling realization in a life of eighty-six years!

JOSEPH REDLICH

The supranational thought, reduced by the developments of the modern centuries to the Danube Monarchy, lay as an inheritance deep in the being of this son of the dynasty. . . . Francis Joseph's political philosophy was old-fashioned, it was a mechanical rather than a living thing, but it operated on a level of the highest morality and ethics.

HEINRICH RITTER VON SRBIK

The revocation of the constitution of 4 March 1849 [by Emperor Francis Joseph] belongs to those acts which are counted among the greatest political mistakes of history—in the ranks of the "lost opportunities."

VIKTOR BIBL

*   *   *

But whoever . . . regards the results of the Compromise [of 1867] from the standpoint of the power interests of the monarchy must confess that the work of Deák and Andrássy has had the most favorable consequences.

EDUARD VON WERTHEIMER

Thus the accomplishment of 1867, after a half century of operating as the basis for dynastic Great Power politics, drove its two creators, the dynasty and the imperial Hungarians, simultaneously with the ruin of German power in Europe, into the abyss.

JOSEPH REDLICH

*   *   *

The nationality conflicts which so adversely affected economic life would in all probability, even without the war, have been modified, had the monarchy continued to exist, into a healthy, productive competition, since the social inequalities which were the actual cause of the evil were rapidly disappearing.

HEINRICH BENEDIKT

Advancing industrialism did not lead to a lasting and healthy consolidation of the existing social structure and of the political dominance [of its leading elements].

HANS ROSENBERG

It would be supremely unjust not to recognize what the Austrian states-men attempted [in an effort] to resolve the problem of nationalities solely because their efforts were not crowned with success. . . . The conviction remains profound and general that . . . that secular community which constituted the Austrian monarchy was necessary, not only to the peoples who inhabited it, but for the good of Europe.

JACQUES DROZ

In view of the now worldwide triumph of nationalism it may appear that the substitution of the Habsburg Empire with nation-states was the course that history had to take in central Europe, too. . . . [Yet] the conflict between nationalism and federalism is still the main, if not necessarily the most visible, internal issue in the Danube region.

STEPHEN BORSODY

I THE MONARCH

The Austrian Empire of 1849 was, by virtue of its size and strategic geographic location, rightful claimant to the status of major European power. Yet it remained far more than the other European powers of its time the product of centuries of successful dynastic combinations. The dynasty, the ruling house, gave a unity to Austria which geatly exceeded the symbolic, impersonal role played by the crown in other European nations. To be sure, the absence of orderly constitutional development on the British or American pattern in any major Continental monarchy assured every king of far greater influence than modern democratic thinking finds acceptable. Yet most contemporary attitudes—republicanism was the faith of a minority in pre-World War I Europe—attributed a directing, often a policy-setting, as well as a symbolic role to the ruler. To what extent Austria's emperor, Francis Joseph, fulfilled the role ascribed to him is therefore vital to understanding the attempts to create a new kind of Austrian unity as the world moved into the era of popular sovereignty.

Joseph Redlich

FRANCIS JOSEPH: BETRAYER OF HIS PEOPLE

Joseph Redlich (1869–1936), lawyer, university professor, former finance minister, was a great admirer of the British parliamentary system, which he had studied extensively. Redlich was intimately familiar with the intricate personal relations of the various political leaders of Austria during the last half of the nineteenth century, a knowledge which he incorporated into his monumental work Das österreichische Reichs: und Staatsproblem, *yet he remained true to the liberal view that strict adherence to orderly constitutional methods is the core of good government. This philosophy underlies his biography of Francis Joseph, from which the following selection is taken.*

When the political earthquake which occurred in Paris in February 1848 shook the political and social order of the Habsburg Empire of Nationalities to its roots, [it brought a new figure to the center of the historic stage]. All in all, the eighteen-year-old archduke on whom the fate of the dynasty depended was a physically and mentally well-endowed youth of the sort one finds among princes' sons, among whom naturally tradition plays a greater role than qualities arising from the individual personality.

Archduke Franzi was certainly not without many talents valuable in the high position for which he was destined, yet [he was] without outstanding intellect; a strong sense of social position and an insistence on proper behavior were distinguishing features of this prince who had scarcely outgrown his boyhood. He lacked any higher intellectual interests; but he balanced this weakness by an unmistakable sense of reality and a sober judgment which he had from the very beginning. He did not appear to his entourage at that time as a particularly kindly nature. His emotional life, quite understandably, was wholly preoccupied in his boyhood by the love and admiration he felt for his mother.

The schoolboy knowledge with which the new emperor marched out of childhood and into adulthood was certainly as good as, perhaps

From Joseph Redlich, *Kaiser Franz Joseph von Österreich: Eine Biographie* (Berlin, 1928), pp. 36–37, 40–45, 52–53, 64, 81–82, 83–100. (English translation published by The Macmillan Company, 1929; following selections are a new translation by the editors.)

FIGURE 1. Emperor Francis Joseph at the time of his marriage to Elizabeth of Bavaria. *(Festgabe der Leipziger Illustrierten Zeitung, 1854)*

better than, that acquired by the sons of the higher nobility, his sole youthful companions. But because his education was broken off when he was still too young, he never received a more serious, scientific education. One must, in this case as in all others, take care not to overestimate the importance of knowledge acquired in school for the actual life pattern of such men who, quite young, are required as heir to fulfill a role of large responsibilities, whether the case in question involves a throne or the administration of extensive estates or large investments. In all these cases the too early assumption of an independent and authoritative position constitutes a real danger for the much envied heir. That Francis Joseph did not escape this danger is perhaps the first of the undeserved yet tragic developments in the life of the future emperor. He was certainly not mature enough to shape, with his own resources, the burden which fate and the requirements of the dynasty, not to speak of the ambition of his proud mother, laid all too soon upon his shoulders. Moreover, the actual practical training of the young archduke as ruler depended on those men who personally influenced him during the first years of his reign and who, through their varied political decisions, unavoidably prescribed the path which he had to follow. They are the actual teachers and instructors of the last powerful emperor of Austria. . . .

In the memorandum of one of the leading officials of the old chancellery, *Hofrat* Hummelauer, one finds a description of the extraordinary circumstances surrounding the accession of Francis Joseph. ". . . After the court arrived in Olmütz [whither it had been transferred from Vienna, which revolutionary disturbances had made untenable], it was necessary to form a new government. Prince Schwarzenberg and Count Stadion were called in. These gentlemen refused to serve Emperor Ferdinand any longer. . . . [But] the political views of the two gentlemen to whom the fate of the monarachy was to be entrusted were not in accord with those of the empress [wife of Ferdinand, who alone could persuade the weak-minded Ferdinand to abdicate]. They wanted to constitutionalize Austria, the empress wanted none of that. . . ." Accordingly, Prince Windisch-Grätz went "bail" for his brother-in-law, the minister-president [Schwarzenberg]. But what the empress had feared, though not expected, occurred. Prince Schwarzenberg changed the abdication proclamation as well as the proclamation of the young monarch in important respects, so that rather than a condemnation of the revolution, this document contained the promise of Archduke Francis to rule constitutionally. At the same time the young archduke adopted the name Francis Joseph, [hoping] in this way to influence public opinion through association with the name of the so-called popular emperor Joseph II, implying the promise of constitutional intentions.

Prince Schwarzenberg [thus] undertook to carry through the abdication of the incompetent emperor, but he broke his promise to the old empress and at the same time cold-bloodedly effected the first great deception of the populace, pronounced in the name of Francis Joseph. For Schwarzenberg himself had not the slightest intention of turning the young archduke now ascending the throne into a constitutional monarch. But he was clever enough to know that the game the court had played under cover of the well-meaning Ferdinand had to be carried on for a while. The spirit of revolution had not been extirpated in Austria, nor had the war begun in September against the revolutionary Hungarian regime been brought to a successful conclusion. Therefore, wholly against the genuinely reactionary wishes of the old empress, the accomplishments of the revolution had for the time being to be guaranteed to the populace.

Schwarzenberg's plan had for its object pacifying the populace of Vienna and the other Austrian cities and generating trust that the new government would publicly acknowledge and carry through the constitutional principle. The peasant masses, as was well known, had been won for the royal house and its antirevolutionary policy ever since the proclamation under Ferdinand of a law canceling peasant dues and eliminating feudal authority over the peasants. . . . Thus Prince Schwarzenberg, when he presented himself and his cabinet to the Reichstag in the session of 27 November [1848]—with the icy calm which was characteristic of him—spoke the words whose actual meaning could have been known only to him and to his few confidants:

> The great work, which it falls to our lot to effect in cooperation with the populace, is the forging of a new bond which will unite all lands and peoples of the monarchy in one great body politic. The administration will not be backward in the search for open-minded popular institutions; on the contrary, it regards it as its duty to place itself in the forefront of this movement. We desire, honestly and without reservation, constitutional monarchy, equality of all citizens before the law, equal rights of all ethnic groups; frankness and accessibility in all branches of the administration shall be the governing principle of the new government. The basis of the free state is the free community!

Thus Schwarzenberg, as he formally acknowledged his cabinet's commitment to liberal government, broke not merely the promise that he had given Prince Windisch-Grätz and the empress but embarked upon a grand deception of the Austrian populace and of the Assembly. . . . Many of the deputies who doubted the sincerity of this formal imperial promise—and there were not a few who had doubts —could find some confirmation of their doubts as early as the next day, when the new monarch replied with some reserve to the words of the president [of the Assembly] at a reception of the delegation sent from the Assembly to the court at Olmütz. Considering that here was the heir to a great empire, scarcely grown out of boyhood and until then always shielded from injustice and from the rest of the world, who began his royal career with a lie of which he must have been conscious, one can appreciate the tragedy which fastened itself on the hitherto guiltless Francis Joseph at this moment and never left him. The old poetic prophecy of the "evil deed which must continuously produce new evil" found here appalling realization in a life of eighty-six years!

There can be no doubt that Francis Joseph did not regard the bad faith vis-à-vis his subjects with which he began his reign as in the slightest degree an error or even a sin: yet one cannot unburden this exceptionally mature and collected youth of the responsibility for grasping the moral significance of what he was doing by simply referring to his youth. True, the deed was not his, but that of Prince Schwarzenberg, who stood by him as his first prime minister. Yet in the deepest core of his being Francis Joseph felt impelled to make this deed his own; he sensed no contradiction [to his previous promises], he expressed no reservations. Prince Schwarzenberg had won his entire trust. He had taught the young archduke that under his, Schwarzenberg's, guidance he could win fame and begin to exercise his sweeping authority. But he must have the strength, the necessary self-confidence, and persistence to effect the will of a true monarch, leading his people against the destructive ideas and goals of the European revolution, against the nonsense of western democracy. That was, right from the beginning, the foundation stone upon which the governing philosophy of Francis Joseph was erected, with which he sought to solve in practice the many tasks that lay before him as ruler. . . .

The return of the court to Vienna [from Olmütz] on 6 May 1849 made possible the creation of Francis Joseph's own court circle, and now he began to develop his own way of life which he continued unchanged for almost seventy years: the strict insistence on a regular pattern of work such as had prevailed in his youth corresponded not merely to the conservative predilections of the heir to the oldest dynasty of Europe but to the inborn qualities of the young monarch, who from boyhood on had regarded regularity, orderliness, and consistency as absolute necessities. The strong sense of duty which Francis Joseph had early exhibited as well as his industry spurred him on to create what he believed to be the necessary conditions of success as a monarch: thoroughness (in supervising all government business which fell to him), reliability (on the part of his immediate associates), and speedy completion (of all assigned tasks). The remarkably good memory with which he was endowed, and which was often admired, frequently came to his aid.

To be sure, the shadow side of his personality was observed by those in his entourage: a certain urgency in settling all matters, a certain reservation towards those individuals who would have preferred a more thorough grounding of his decisions [in contrast] to the speed [which he preferred] and who let their opinions become known. But the chief defect of his personality was a total lack of imagination. Such individuals are always extremely unsympathetic towards any departures from the accustomed way of doing things. This goes hand in hand with a certain overestimation of the value of old forms and practical rules which inevitably leads, sooner or later, to the condition in which content loses significance while old forms and traditions linger on. . . . Yet even in court life, otherwise so conservative, the year 1848 had made some changes: the greatest change lay in the fact that henceforth the young emperor, for whom his army had won back his capital, saw himself first and foremost as commander in chief. And thus it was, with the accession of Francis Joseph, that the military element entered into the foreground of the Vienna court. . . . Undeniably, this was not so much the fault of *General-adjutant* Count Grünne and the young officers of the emperor's suite, for nothing else was to be expected from them. This severe reproach belongs exclusively to a man who could have foreseen the dangers of such a final development in the training of Francis Joseph. This man was Prince Schwarzenberg, the prime minister and actual founder of the new imperial glory of Francis Joseph. . . . He was the man who directed the whole policy of the empire from the day his cabinet was formed to the day of his death. He was the only man who controlled everything at the court and to whom the emperor listened as to no other. Consequently the historical responsibility falls to Schwarzenberg alone for the practical training of the young monarch as well as for the effect which the political actions of the prime minister had on the governing philosophy of the ruler. . . . For Schwarzenberg had made his program known in this respect in clear and succinct terms as early as his introductory speech to the Reichstag at Kremsier as well as in the young emperor's manifesto upon ascending the throne: the Habsburg lands should form a new unity, a new empire should be created in which there was no place for the historic constitution of Hungary. And for this reason Hungary had to be conquered. . . .

Yet before Francis Joseph had sent the Russian czar his appeal for help [in suppressing the Hungarian revolution, which the imperial army had failed to subdue] he carried through with his own hand a deed which would certainly have deeply offended the czar, had the latter not already been fully instructed as to the objectives of Schwarzenberg. On the fourth of March 1849 the Reichstag, the popular assembly [created during the revolution] whose constitutional committee had drafted a constitution after two months of strenuous work, was dissolved by imperial order. At the same time, however, a new imperial constitution, arising wholly from the sovereignty of the emperor, was proclaimed. This legislative accomplishment had been carried through in total secrecy during three months of unceasing consultation by the Schwarzenberg ministry. The new constitution drew in many respects on the creative concepts of the Reichstag committee, which was simultaneously debating [the same problems], although it incorporated noteworthy departures from the outspokenly democratic principles of the majority of the Reichstag committee. This constitution, forced upon the Austrian people, proposed a well-thought-out liberal system: it was principally different from the draft of Kremsier [created by the Reichstag], in that it covered the whole empire, whereas the Reichstag had from the beginning merely attempted to draw up a constitution for the western parts of the empire: the traditional German provinces, the lands of the Bohemian crown, Galicia, and the Adriatic coastal provinces, which were to be incorporated into a unitary state. . . .

Thus a new regime began in Austria with the publication of the constitution, which can scarcely be matched in the consciously deceptive character inherent in it even in that era of bold and skilled concealment of reaction. The new, unified empire, at first established, on paper at least, as a constitutional monarchy and introduced to the world as such, was from then on "provisionally" ruled in strictly absolutist fashion by the Schwarzenberg ministry. Numerous laws were elaborated in the various branches of the government, thoroughly debated in the ministerial council, and then promulgated by the emperor as "provisional" laws. The whole of the central administration, of the court system, of the local administration, of the tax and impost system, and soon also of the school system was rebuilt from the bottom up in well-planned legislative projects, which in their individual parts always kept in mind their relationship to the whole as well as to the final purpose: to build up anew a thoroughly unified governmental authority in the empire. And yet all that at first formed nothing but a great question mark because the government let it be known that all these laws, originating exclusively in the total sovereignty of the emperor, must later be evaluated and then finally authorized as laws by the central [legislative] authority [created by] the new constitution. . . .

What the end of this game would be, even Schwarzenberg and his trusted helper could not at that moment say. For no one could foresee that Vienna and the provinces, which in the year 1848 had with one blow become the scene of wild revolution, would show themselves, as they did, so permanently subservient to the new regime of Prince Schwarzenberg—a regime that based itself on military power. The unique quality of the play was, therefore, that this first modern manipulator of power in central Europe, Prince Schwarzenberg, surrounded himself with an assortment of outstanding liberal statesmen; and these men worked unceasingly for two years and more to create liberal and modern laws, whose precise execution they supervised through the persons of first-class provincial administrators, many partly bourgeois in origin. At the same time this government preserved a strict state of siege in Vienna and Prague, it set up throughout Austria a completely new power apparatus—for [the benefit of] the emperor and the central government—the militarily organized gendarmerie, with an initial strength of sixteen regiments, which in its technical equipment, in its admirable discipline, and in the extent of its police functions created something quite new for the empire and for central Europe. . . .

One can read the sharpest attacks on Schwarzenberg and on the liberalism of his legislation and administration in the letters of the old Prince Metternich to his friend, President of the *Hofkammer* [the court council] *Freiherr* von Kübeck, as well as in the latter's answers. . . . And now this same man appeared on the stage having contributed not a little to the preparations for the new accession [of Francis Joseph in place of Ferdinand]. Henceforth he advocated the strongest reaction against the ideas of 1848 and the basic tendencies of the Stadion constitution of 4 March 1849 and emerged in the front row of the advisers of the emperor. It is not altogether clear whether Schwarzenberg and Alexander Bach may not have toyed with the thought of carrying on an attempt at a kind of pseudoliberal constitutional regime. . . . But the decisive fact was that *Freiherr* von Kübeck presented the young emperor with a plan for the formal setting aside of the constitution as well as for the establishment of an undisguised autocracy and met the comparable aims of the emperor. . . . August [saw] the publication of the Proclamations of 20 August 1851, which rested on the supreme sovereignty of the emperor and in which the program of autocracy already appears in words that are legally unmistakable. The essential part of this program was the solemn abolition of the principle of ministerial responsibility. . . .

Francis Joseph did not know that the autocracy which Kübeck had created for him was something quite new in Austria, that it, along with the unified empire, actually signified a new revolution from above, if carried through in a rightward direction, for the benefit of the person of the emperor: a true coup d'état. . . . In this whole area [of authority] only the will of the emperor had significance and scope, unrestricted by any right[s] of the citizen, who should remain exclusively subject. On the one side the people, politically without rights, on the other the emperor, who with his army, his ministers, and administrators would produce the prosperity of the whole empire through their apolitical government assuring the best for all: that was the picture of the future. . . .

Heinrich Ritter von Srbik

FRANCIS JOSEPH: SYMBOL OF IMPERIAL UNITY

The outstanding figure among modern Austrian historians is undeniably Heinrich Ritter von Srbik (1878–1951). Though many find Srbik's assertion of the continued validity of the supranational state idea embodied in the Holy Roman Empire unacceptable, none can deny the meticulousness of his historical scholarship nor his feeling for the deeper currents of history. His evaluation of Francis Joseph, from which the following selection has been taken, has been described by a contemporary scholar as "the best short appreciation of Francis Joseph's personality."[1]

Before the war [of 1914–1918] the figure of the aging emperor Francis Joseph was for millions of Austrians the symbol of the entire country, simultaneously a dual "nation" and a single entity, a symbol both of its inner nature and of its exterior status as a Great Power; a symbol of that which held together in a single structured community a body which was doing battle on many fronts with the changing currents of the times. . . .

Now Francis Joseph who has been dead a full generation, has become an historical figure. The foundations of life for the older generations in both Austria and Germany have been overturned, new notions of life and new forms of existence are arising from a nameless confusion, new points of view have developed from the collapse of the monarchic-constitutional system in central Europe, from the end of the old Danube Empire and from the death of the Bismarckian Empire, from the emergence of the will of the masses and the countervailing influences of the historical forces still operative among the assorted peoples [of this area].

The contradictory descriptions of the character and governing

From Heinrich Ritter von Srbik, "Franz Joseph I. Charakter und Regierungsgrundsätze," in *Aus Österreichs Vergangenheit* (Salzburg, 1949), pp. 221–241. The original essay was composed as a speech presented at the *Kulturbund* in Vienna on 10 February 1931 and before the *Deutsche Gesellschaft 1914* in Berlin on 5 March 1931. Translated by permission of Hans Heinrich Ritter von Srbik.

[1] Adam Wandruszka [professor of history, University of Cologne], *The House of Habsburg*, trans. Cathleen and Hans Epstein (Garden City, 1964), p. 162.

principles of the old emperor which have appeared since the collapse of the old world, mirror the ferment of the times. A taste for sensationalism, a lack of knowledge, and a spirit of hate directed some pens, producing repelling and superficial distortions. The nationalistic tendencies of the successor states and the war-guilt legend among the victors [of 1918] victimized the monarch who, in fact, was a ruler with a strong desire for justice and peace. Joseph Redlich's highly respectable scholarly work renders judgments based on the failure of a long reign and on prejudices derived from observing a slowly crumbling and finally dying [imperial] Austria. It presents the negative conclusion that Francis Joseph never learned to understand the leading ideas of his time and was guilty of failing to undertake a timely reconstruction of Austria-Hungary into a union of national democracies. On the other side, respect for the dead and for his country and indignation at a flood of false accusations evoked a defense which occasionally forgot the limits of the defensible, and the few attempts to grasp the true personality [of Francis Joseph] in the framework of his times and to test this against the rules of historical significance have generally been disregarded as purely academic productions of partisan viewpoints.

A life of eighty-six years on this planet stands before our eyes, sixty-eight years spent ruling an old European Great Power, helping to create, and at the same time suffering with, an epoch which extends from the stormy year of 1848 to the middle of one of the greatest conflicts between nations and peoples. Francis Joseph was one of the shapers and leaders of this period, a period incomparably rich in experience, an era which ushered in vast alterations in the political, national, social, and economic structure of the Continent, but he was at the same time victim of the national and liberal tendencies [which manifested themselves] during his long life. Is it not, therefore, a challenging task, to try to reconstruct this being, to relive through this historical personality the issues of historic greatness and historic tragedy, to define the task and the qualities available to meet it, to ascertain the general trends of the time and the unique characteristics of the individual out of whose interaction history is formed? . . .

If one tries to grasp the whole of Francis Joseph's intellectual and moral qualities, one recognizes at once certain enduring characteristics typical of his distinguished family heritage, as well as qualities which, although present from the beginning, first acquired decisive significance as a result of experience. To the end of his life Emperor Francis Joseph remained a complete cavalier of the old school, a living example of knightly ideals, personally brave, as he revealed at [the battle of] St. Lucia [near Verona, in May 1848], at the bridge of Raab [in Hungary], after Solferino, and at the assassination attempt of Libenyi; a man honorable and correct to his fingertips, punctual and painfully punctilious almost to the point of pedantry, tactful and wholly untouched by court flattery. He held firm to a very personal notion of respectability in political as well as in military struggles and labeled as "scandalous" developments in the political and diplomatic world which offended his enduring principles of morality and order: a quite atypical way of judging the effects and consequences of the principles and [conflicting] interests of the states, peoples, and groups [of his world] and of their leaders. . . . The dignity which lay in his person did not long for popularity, but rather regarded the acclaim of the people as the appropriate tribute [due his rank] and regarded the absence of such acclaim as disrespect. . . .

Such observations years ago induced his contemporaries to think that the gift of emotion was lacking in the emperor. True, he was not sentimental, never yielding [to emotional pressure], he never let himself be overwhelmed by exterior impressions and was able to continue working even in the face of the most appalling blows of fate, such as the hanging of his brother Max [by the republican forces in Mexico], the suicide of his only son, the murder of his wife. He revealed early signs of hardness, of self-containment and mistrust, of a severity apparently untempered by love in questions of military or political affairs. . . . The key to this riddle of his personal qualities can be found in his conception of majesty: he always differentiated sharply between his public and his private life. It was not only that he was called "Your Majesty" and that he possessed all the natural exterior attributes of majesty; the concept of majesty was rooted deep in his being, and he, who even in his letters to his mother seldom touched on his inner life, remained so convinced of the lonely elevation of the Habsburg throne that this conviction gradually isolated him from human contact. Once he not merely felt but showed deep pain—at the death of [his first prime minister,] Prince Schwarzenberg; thereafter he opened up his inner being to no others in his entourage, not even his friends, changed his statesmen like used up instruments, allowed even those closest to him, like his youthful playmate Count Taaffe or his old military comrade of many decades, Count Beck, to be thrown out of office and consequently out of close association with him, apparently without the slightest emotional twinge. . . . Too great popularity among his statesmen appeared to him to diminish the dignity of the crown, even where there was no question of personal ambition, and a handshake from the emperor was for an ordinary citizen a quite extraordinary honor. The ancient imperial concept overshadowed all else, an inheritance of the centuries, much older than the Austrian imperial crown, blocking the emperor's original receptivity to the world; he became ever more impersonal, ever more merely the embodiment of government. . . .

One must acknowledge in this figure of strong nerves endowed with a powerful memory a lack of imaginative fantasy. And this lack of soaring fantasy characterized his political and military leadership of the state. He had a great capacity for looking the realities of life in the face, for sacrificing old ideals without complaint, however painful it may have been to him privately; he possessed the skill of recognizing that which was possible in politics and of pursuing it with intelligence; he possessed also the talents of an outstanding official of the old school and understood the significance of the sentence *"minima non curat praetor"* [the high official does not concern himself with little things] and took it to heart. In the later stages of his career he could decide all kinds of special questions with authority, on the basis of his incomparable knowledge of the affairs of state, and he brought his official authority to bear in individual matters, such as the introduction of universal suffrage in 1906. But it was not given to him to be able to envisage in any substantial measure unborn potentialities, those still existing as ideas only. He was not among those of whom Hegel said that the concealed spirit of history, lurking in them, was pounding at the door of the present and demanding admittance.

Basically, Francis Joseph was never a man of strong initiative. Buried underneath his exterior of unapproachable, definitive majesty there lay a distaste for final decisions, and a tendency towards cautious postponement until honor and the ultimate raison d'état, the sole factors determining his readiness to attempt something new, compelled him to act and made further circumvention impossible. In the early years of his public life this quality was not nearly so noticeable as in the later years of his career. . . . At the beginning of his reign, trusting in the fresh powers of his imperial will and his political authority, he ascended the throne with bold faith in Austria and in his dynasty, supported by a strong-willed mother and a statesman of uncommon drive. . . . [As he grew older] he grew more adaptable, without changing his deepest, most personal views. In the case of this political realist one cannot speak of an ideology, merely of the basic outlines of a philosophy which with him was more instinctive than based on any clear rationale. . . . The supranational thought, reduced by the developments of the modern centuries to the Danube Monarchy, lay as an inheritance deep in the being of this son of the dynasty which through many generations had stood at the head of the Holy Roman Empire, which had married the universal, Christian imperial idea of the Middle Ages with faith in its dynastic mission as a great power, and which had made of the "universal state" with its narrower power base a central European Great Power.

Francis Joseph's sense of a central European mission was thus deeply rooted in the past. We should not overrate it, should not discern in it too much "geopolitics"—as has happened—but it is certainly true that this emperor ascribed to the center of the Continent an assured and historically necessary role in opposition to the flanking powers of Russia and France. Consequently the Habsburg monarchy was to him a natural, unquestionable whole in terms of the conditions created by nature in the center of the Continent. . . . Can one then, in view of this universal, central European and Austrian conception [of Austria] with its traditional German overtones, accept the current judgment that the emperor never rose above a purely dynastic, patrimonial concept of the state, never got beyond the point of a feudal sense of family responsibility? Surely, the dynastic element was so deeply rooted in him that the sense of the identity, of the indissoluble union, of the House of Habsburg and the Austrian Empire was for him an article of faith. But this faith was far more than a mere sense of private property to be husbanded, it was rooted in an old historic viewpoint and its possessor was ennobled by an unerring sense of responsibility and a code of honor, with its primary emphasis on duty, not on rights. Francis Joseph's political philosophy was old-fashioned, it was a mechanical rather than a living thing, but it operated on a level of the highest morality and ethics. . . .

Despite the crumbling of the structure which had been built on these foundations, the essential outlines of this concept of the state remained intact during his long, incomparably eventful life. . . . The lesson of the year 1859 convinced him of the need, however contrary to his personal philosophy, of introducing constitutional forms into his empire; he sought tentatively the correct road, that of the federalistic October Diploma, then that of the centralistic February Patent of Schmerling, later the constitutional suspension of Belcredi, and finally the special compromise with Hungary, but always with a view to the effect on foreign affairs. . . . To see states, as Ranke and Bismarck did, as vast living beings, with conflicting life interests and each with its own unique nature in need of expression was a gift never conferred upon him. . . . His state fell victim to the ceaseless drive of the nationalities [to win independent self-expression]; but his realization that the undiluted principle of the national state could not be introduced in central Europe without severe losses and his understanding of the central role of the Germans as the backbone of an east-central European Austrian state remain valid. . . .

He always saw the role of the monarch as above the peoples, not [as mediator] among them. . . . As at the beginning of his reign, as in 1860 when he announced his determination after issuing the October Diploma to "keep the power in his [own] hands," in the same way the old man remained firmly convinced that the unity of Austria had to be incorporated in the person of the monarch, and he was never free of the skepticism that the dual state, or even the non-Hungarian half of the empire, was completely unsuited for a constitution in the western European pattern or for a parliamentary system [similar to those in the West]. [Nonetheless], although he remained personally antiliberal, he allowed liberal ministries and liberal parliamentary majorities of the "kingdoms and lands represented in the Reichsrat" to rule, for the sake of the state until they exhausted their usefulness. However, he held firm to the not inconsiderable remnants of his personal authority: he continued to regard as a political necessity the direct and indirect influence of the emperor in the negotiations of the parties, in the operations of the ministries, and on individual politicians; and this influence remained a practical reality, however firmly he held fast to the letter of his constitutional responsibilities.

Once again his ability to efface his own person and views without sacrificing his major principles stands out in the transformation from autocrat to personal creator of universal suffrage. The emperor was motivated by hope that, for the sake of state and dynasty, the conflict of nationalities might be brought to an end, perhaps even by the realization that the political advance of the popular masses was not to be halted; still, behind all that remained the primacy of Austria's responsibility as a Great Power, which lent inner unity to all the variegated experiments in governmental form. This latter [responsibility] also dictated the ruler's relations with Hungary, his reaction to all the efforts [of the Hungarians] to stultify the authority of the imperial officers. The army and foreign policy, those were the areas which even in Hungary the ruler retained as crown rights, however strictly he held to the spirit of the constitutional rules in Hungary after 1867.

And here we enter that area of the greatest tragedy of this man, greater than the loss in European territory and respect. The will to embark upon a promising renewal of this complex state structure, to seek out an acceptable and lasting solution of the Austrian and Austro-Hungarian question [under the slogan] "variety in unity," was his best feature, but his personal qualities were simply inadequate for this admittedly unbelievably complicated task, despite all the wisdom and the incomparable self-sacrifice which he exhibited. It was, in fact, never given to the emperor to find total solutions, and he grew weary and frayed from the never-ending effort to find through assorted schemes merely a partial cure for the disease. Dualism was in 1867 a necessity of the moment, but it ought not to have immobilized the empire and brought about the isolation of two governmental systems, whose fates were fundamentally bound up with one another. The political dominance of the Magyars in the kingdom of St. Stephen could not be maintained by artificial means; still less could the Germans in Austria master the task of holding together and directing the people in view of the elementary force of ethnic majorities which unquestionably enjoyed a full and rich cultural life in the monarchy, but which were not appeased [thereby] politically. Only "centralistic federalism," to use a phrase of the former premier Clam-Martinic, could produce a cure, provided the medication did not come from outside and [was not stamped] with German centralistic tendencies. In no other way could the monarchy do justice to its central European role as a state of many peoples under German cultural and political leadership.

In this really crucial and basic question of Austrian and central European life, Francis Joseph's personality revealed itself as too weak. He gave vastly of himself, to the point of exhausting his strength, he put all his rich experience at the service of a kind of rearguard effort holding off the destructive forces, but he retreated before the historically based opposition of the Germans and the Magyars [to accepting a less important role for themselves]; he feared the quite probably bloody struggle which was entailed in the dilemma of "kill or cure," as in the case of a serious operation. All his efforts remained in their initial phase, and he finally let things go on as they would, seeking only to avoid the worst. In his person inertia came to take the place of the necessary dynamism. . . .

It is as if a curious crippling overtook Francis Joseph in his later years, a pessimism which suspected a scarcely avoidable, tragic fate; a feeling of representing a powerful past, which was not able to come to terms with the present; a sensing of the way to a new period of life for state and dynasty, and an oppressing fear of not finding the way with certainty nor of being able to follow it to the end. He incorporated the tradition of an old-style monarch with the awareness that history had entered a new era; he felt himself to be the protector of ancient tradition and of the inherited forces in state and society and saw that the new things, the people and the nation, were winning out; he was aware of the historical mission of the Danubian monarchy, he knew also that the task of this empire was [to create] a peaceful, supranational union of peoples in a geographic entity, but he could not quite grasp this fruitful idea for renewing the old state, and still less envisage it in a concrete sense. . . .

But is his person only a representation of the past? Is his sole historical role that of representing a disappearing type belonging to past centuries, looking always backwards and hesitantly giving way to the overpowering forces of a new era, in the creation of which he played no actual part? Is his historical significance to be found solely in the conflicts of his dogged resistance to the national, the liberal, the democratic idea, his struggles with the political power of the higher bourgeoisie, of the lower middle class, finally of the politicized mob, and in his giving way to these irresistible pressures? In my opinion we do not in this way exhaust the significance of the matter.

An historical personality has to be measured not merely against that which he accomplished but against that which he aspired to do, and when a long life has served as the propagator of indestructible ideas it retains its proper place, exceeding the importance of actual accomplishment. However little Francis Joseph contained the spark of genius in himself, however much he pursued a policy of sober dynastic politics foreign to the primacy of The People, still a higher worth lent dignity to this policy and its supporters through the enduring ideas [which they represented]. This last representative of Habsburg universalism in its more limited, modern, central European form was always aware that for east-central Europe the equation of state and nation is impractical and that, regarded as a whole, that part of the world had to be organized into a union of national *and* supranational entities. He was justifiably of the opinion that Austria was basically the most acceptable system for a peaceful cohabitation of many small ethnic groups in an area held together by its geographic unity. He was not able to solve the riddle of what kind of Austrian state could provide the framework for this joint tenancy, but he understood that the only lasting solution to its problems lay in a central Europe led by the Austro-Germans. He kept alive in his state the mission of the Germans to spread German culture of the Austrian variety in southeastern Europe, at the same time making it possible for the other nationalities to develop their own cultural life and to realize in the fullest degree yet seen respect for national minorities. Can a human existence be counted among the unproductive, whose operative ideas, however incomplete their realization, have deep roots in the past and, as it seems to us, point towards a better future?

II THE CONSTITUTION

For all the many differences which divided them, conservatives and liberals of the mid-nineteenth century shared the view that the vital issues of the day were constitutional. Thus the solution to Austria's problems had to be found in governmental reconstruction. Yet whether this reconstruction was to take the form of a new view of the empire, a building from the ground up of community responsibility after the manner of the Stein reforms in Prussia during the Napoleonic era, or the creation of a central legislative body, filled with representatives of the various principalities and social classes which composed the empire, remained in dispute. Three distinct phases of constitutional experimentation remain, however, indisputable: the Schwarzenberg reforms of 1849–1851, the Schmerling reforms of 1860–1861, and the Compromise of 1867.

Phase I: Centralism

The restoration of Austrian monarchical authority, after the 1848 revolutionaries appeared to have ended it forever, must have seemed to the new ruler and his advisors something of a modern miracle. Yet both monarch and advisors remained true to the traditions of the enlightened emperor Joseph II, attempting to forestall the future by introducing from above those reforms which appeared to be most in demand from below. Underlying this approach lay the belief that the demand for liberal institutions, liberal limitations on the monarchy, could be defused by cutting out the old inefficiency of government, by abolishing medieval survivals. In this attempt to make economy and efficiency in government a substitute for effective parliamentary institutions, Austria was no different from all the other major European powers of that time. But in Austria the as yet unrestricted sovereignty of the emperor was used to carry through reforms which would create, working from the center out, a government which would primarily serve the needs of the liberal elements, in which all the parts fit neatly together, which was, in short, something of a "modern major general."

Heinrich Friedjung
STADION AND COMMUNITY RESPONSIBILITY

The reformers of the Schwarzenberg government were stirred by a vision of a vast central European empire stretching from the Baltic to the Adriatic. Yet the government which touches the average citizen, and which must bear primary responsibility for evoking his loyalty, is the local government; and in the view of Heinrich Friedjung (1851–1920), student of Germany's most famous academic historians of the nineteenth century, Leopold Ranke and Theodor Mommsen, liberal journalist and politician, the core of the Schwarzenberg reconstruction lay in the ideas of Francis Stadion for the reform of local government. Although Friedjung is more widely known as the author of The Struggle for Supremacy in Germany, *his uncompleted* Oesterreich von 1848 bis 1860 *reveals an intimate and judicious knowledge of the events of the mid-nineteenth century.*

Schwarzenberg [the minister-president] knew himself well enough to realize that he needed a helper to fill out the gaps in his knowledge.

From Heinrich Friedjung, *Oesterreich von 1848 bis 1860* (Stuttgart and Berlin, 1908), Vol. I, pp. 97–102, 135–38. Translated by permission of J. G. Cotta'sche Buchhandlung.

For this purpose only two men were possible: [Alexander] Bach and, even more desirable, Count Francis Stadion. The latter came from one of the first families of the empire, but embodied a type of the Austrian aristocrat in sharp contrast to that of Schwarzenberg and Windisch-Grätz. He knew very precisely the needs of the state from the experience garnered at his previous post as provincial president [*Statthalter*] in Triest and Galicia, as well as from serious studies [of governmental problems], and had his own complete reform program, the execution of which formed his life's task. His strict monarchistic views made him a not unworthy spiritual associate of the conservative reformer in the manner of Stein and Robert Peel. Stadion was also in Olmütz [with the remainder of the court], and since his specialized knowledge clearly outshone that of the other advisors of the court, including Schwarzenberg, his opinion won out, at first, against the representatives of absolutism. . . . He recommended preserving constitutional forms [despite the second revolution in Vienna], and allowing the Reichstag [conceded by the government in the spring] to continue its work [in drafting a constitution]. Schwarzenberg yielded at first, since he could not deny the weighty arguments of Stadion, even if this concession was in his eyes nothing but temporary tactics. . . .

Otherwise the cabinet devoted its efforts to finding a middle position between the [contending] parties. It transferred the Austrian Reichstag from Vienna to the Moravian provincial town of Kremsier, in the vicinity of Olmütz, where Schwarzenberg presented a program to it on 27 November in which the government spoke out "honestly and without reservation" in favor of constitutional monarchy. Stadion's ideas and recommendations set the tone of every sentence in this document which was greeted with acclamation. . . .

[For] the outstanding figure of the government was the minister of the interior, Count Stadion; therefore his centralistic and liberal ideas were decisive. His plan was, after the elimination of the earlier court chancelleries of Hungary and the Siebenbürgen, to create a unified government with a representative assembly containing deputies from all kingdoms and lands [of the empire], east as well as west. . . . His original plan was to come to an agreement over the new constitution with the Reichstag which had been transferred to Kremsier and whose dissolution he had forestalled; in this way the ideas of Joseph II, which guided him as well as Bach, should achieve realization.

Sladion.

FIGURE 2. Count Francis Stadion, who devised the first scheme for imperial constitutional reconstruction. *(From the picture archives of the Austrian National Library)*

In the key question of Austrian constitutional law, the relationship of the empire to the individual lands, Stadion had a grandiose, though not very practical, plan. He wanted to restrict the local spirit of the provinces and therefore [proposed] to divide the monarchy into counties [*Kreise*], after the pattern of the French departments. In order not to wound the sensitivities of the various nationalities, the county boundaries should be constructed as far as possible to coincide with the language boundaries; within these narrow confines a freer unfolding of the national spirits would be possible and was anticipated by Stadion. His wide-ranging mind went [however] well beyond the unbending centralism of France, for he believed it to be highly desirable that in all the lower levels of the administration, in the local communities, in the districts, and in the counties, a larger measure of autonomy should be provided for. For him this was no information device, merely to find out what the special wishes of the nationalities and the provinces might be, but rather a most promising practical necessity. Consequently the local government law of 17 March 1849, drafted by Stadion, went far beyond any contemporary pattern in providing the right of self-government on the three lower levels of the administration, the communities, the districts, and the counties. It was in this sense that he had inserted in the program of the Schwarzenberg government of 27 November 1848 the sentence: "the free community is the basis of the free state."

Stadion was, however, well aware that the historical division of the empire into kingdoms and lands had become too ingrained to be thrown out without any further ado. Therefore, he believed, one had to leave provincial presidencies [*Statthaltereien*] in existence as an administrative expression of their historic unity. The authority of the presidents should, however, be narrowly circumscribed, because it was not the crown lands but rather the counties which were intended to bear the main responsibility for the administration. Once the new system had, with time, been accepted, so the minister said, the provincial presidencies, which were superfluous, could be abolished.

Since Stadion at the same time, even if only temporarily, also ran the education ministry, it was possible for him to bring to the higher and middle schools some of that free spirit [which activated him]. During the revolution Undersecretary Ernst von Feuchtersleben had served as the head of the education administration, one of the finest brains of Metternich's Austria. Under Stadion's leadership, and on the basis of von Feuchtersleben's plan, the reorganization of the universities and the high schools [*Gymnasien*] was carried through. This work had been virtually completed by Exner and Benitz when Count Leo Thun took office as education minister.

For the reform of the internal administration Stadion had first and foremost a thoroughly knowledgeable and capable helper in Joseph Oettl, whose advice, during his earlier service in provincial administration in Lemberg, he had never failed to follow. This modest and thoroughly competent man performed major services as head of the central administration in the Ministry of the Interior under Stadion and [later] under Bach.

It is surprising what a quantity of inspiration Count Stadion exuded during his mere half year of office, and so much the more as during this period the destructive brain disease to which he fell victim, all too soon for the good of the state, was already developing. When he entered office his nerves were already in such a frayed condition that he could bring himself to work only under artificial stimulants—and as a result destroyed his nervous system that much sooner. He had much to accomplish and foresaw too little time for it. In his drive for achievement he overlooked the difficulties inherent in his plan to reduce Hungary to a province in a unified state. His plans were large in conception, yet had too little regard for the power of tradition and the preference for local customs. Nonetheless it would have been possible to carry out his plans, at least in their basic form, in the lands west of the Leitha [River] had the government carried on with them consistently. This was not true in Hungary—that country could only have been held under the control of the central government by force, and the Magyars would always have tried to revolt under favorable circumstances. . . .

Richard Charmatz
BRUCK AND ECONOMIC UNITY

Richard Charmatz (b. 1879), journalist and editor of the liberal Neue Freie Presse *of Vienna, devoted a long career to observing Austrian public affairs. Author of a number of books on Austrian history under Emperor Francis Joseph, his biography of* Freiherr von Bruck *emphasizes the vital importance of the economic unification of the empire which the Schwarzenberg reforms made possible.*

In the struggle for the creation of a central European economic unit which Bruck carried through with élan and persistence, insight and idealism, he achieved the stature of a path-breaking personality. The effects of his labors can be seen far beyond the borders of Austria; the richness and forcefulness of his ideas embraced all of central Europe.

From Richard Charmatz, *Minister Freiherr von Bruck: Der Vorkämpfer Mitteleuropas* (Leipzig, 1916), pp. 41–43, 52–54. Translated by permission of S. Hirzel Verlag Kg.

The manner in which Bruck attempted to find a solution for the most important problem of his time, the German question, made of him a statesman, the outstanding spokesman of a great and promising idea.

On a later occasion the minister of commerce proudly laid claim to the authorship of this concept of economic union. In 1846 he spoke out against the dangers of a separate German Customs Union. Two years later, when the revolution broke out in Germany, he made economic union his article of faith. In [the National Assembly in] Frankfurt he joined no party, but remained above all groups. . . . That was his outstanding service, that he placed economic necessities in the foreground, that he valued the pressures of economic forces. The age of cabinet politics appeared in 1848 to be over, but how should popular politics be made effective? Bruck found a new formula, which he adapted to the needs of the nation, the state, and the princes. Germany molded into an economic unit, extended to a central European union, Austria and Prussia linked harmoniously—what an enticing concept! And not only the German problem could be solved this way. Firmly embedded in the larger framework [of a central European union], Austria would become the master of all her domestic problems. Bruck's idea was inspired, truly statesmanlike—too significant for the period in which it was to be realized. . . .

Still, the difficulties to be surmounted could not be overlooked. In Austria and in the Customs Union different tariff structures as well as different tax, monopoly, and currency regulations prevailed. The Germans regarded the lightly patrolled Austrian border with distrust, a condition which promoted smuggling. The paper currency of the Danube Monarchy also did little to inspire confidence. A method of dividing up the customs revenue, which would be necessary in a fusion, was hard to work out. An additional problem was provided by the divergence of the institutions in the two halves of the empire; for an interior customs line created two separate commercial entities within it, which were united into a whole only in their relations with foreign nations. Yet what were these obstacles, really, to a man of Bruck's energy? Since early 1848 the course of development had quickened, and innovations were easier to bring to fruition than people had previously thought possible. . . .

When Bruck published his significant plan [in October 1849], assorted measures [which could serve as preliminaries] had already been introduced. Early in the year a commission had been called into

FIGURE 3. Carl Freiherr von Bruck, who hoped through economic integration to build a modern Austrian Empire. *(From the picture archives of the Austrian National Library)*

being, with the task of reconstructing the customs system. An experienced official, Professor Baumgartner, served as chairman; the research lay in the hands of Hock. In this way the serious intention of the monarchy was made known, namely, that it wished to break with the system of economic isolation and to create the preconditions for a customs union with Germany. In June the Ministerial Council met to consider when the interior customs line dividing Austria and Hungary into two separate commercial units should be abolished. The members expressed themselves in favor of prompt action, since paragraph 7 of the March constitution had already assured that the empire formed a single customs and trading unit. An imperial patent issued in October laid the basis for the abolition of the tax privileges in Hungary and for equal taxation on both sides of the Leitha [separating Austria and Hungary]. All these measures made no small contribution towards the creation of the 70-million-man customs union. Bruck's article established the principle that neither side in a customs union of Germany and Austria should enjoy special advantages at the expense of the other. It stressed the need for reform in the three great German commercial groups: the Habsburg Empire, the German Customs Union, and the north German coastal states [which did not belong to the Customs Union]. Union should follow according to an established plan, not with a single leap. Bruck proposed four stages. The first and most important period would be dedicated to domestic customs reform, preparation for the reconciliation, and fusion of the various interests and would at the same time lay the groundwork for further development. With the beginning of the fourth stage essentially free trade should already be established in *Mitteleuropa.* The final and decisive step, the introduction of complete economic unification, would have to follow according to special agreements. Still, for a specific period equalization duties, so far as they might be needed, could continue to exist. Bruck stressed that minor reservations should not act as a deterrent to such promising beginnings; "the natural law of development" demanded compliance. . . .

A few days later the newspaper [*Austria*] reported that nowhere had a significant voice been raised against either the proposals or the principles underlying them. Yet they [such voices] were to be found, especially in the rest of Germany. One must be prepared for attacks from two quarters, from the one-sided, abstract-minded free traders and from the party favoring a small Germany [without Austria]. At the end of this article in a semiofficial journal are the following sentences: "Whether or not the common interest makes desirable the later creation of an advising and voting central authority is a question each must decide for himself. In any case, enticing prospects are now more than ever before seriously bound up with the customs question, whose solution would accomplish more than all previous draft constitutions." That was said in late fall 1849, a time therefore in which the reaction was already certain of its victory and parliamentarianism was already defeated. Bruck, however, knew the longing of the populace, and he therefore made mention of the fact that customs union would be a means whereby this longing could be brought closer to fulfillment. The Augsburg *Allgemeine Zeitung,* the protagonist [among the press] of the Habsburg monarchy in South Germany, had already published a hymn of praise: "The idea is a magnificent one, unimaginably fruitful and significant for Germany and Austria. Its realization is a necessity, if one wants to insure the greatness and power of these empires, and the welfare of their peoples, if one wants to create, in the satisfaction of their needs, a lasting and healthy form." The Austrian industrialists reacted in a much more reserved fashion. They didn't dash to join the minister of commerce [Bruck], they didn't rush out to help him. From fear of what was new [in his proposal], they preferred not to abandon the comfortable old system. Its restrictions didn't bother them, they preferred the old protection to the fresh, enticing, promising competition of a larger system. On the other hand the minister of commerce had the satisfaction [of knowing] that the General German Union for the Protection of National Labor, in which the German manufacturers were organized, came out forcefully in favor of his scheme. . . .

Viktor Bibl

IMPERIAL RECONSTRUCTION: THE GRAND DECEPTION

Viktor Bibl (1870–1947), devoted democrat and professor at the University in Vienna, could find nothing good in the Schwarzenberg reforms. Like Redlich, he believed the betrayal of the government's promise to create representative institutions sabotaged all popular trust in the imperial government. Only the acceptance of the constitution drafted by the popular representatives in the National Assembly, whose creation the revolutionaries of 1848 had wrung from the reluctant imperial government, could have assured popular good will. In failing to adopt this Kremsier constitution, so called after the Moravian provincial center in which the Assembly's later meetings were held, the imperial government lost its last opportunity to bring the Habsburg monarchy into harmony with the irresistible drive for popular sovereignty.

Count Stadion was, of course, in fact quite serious about self-government in province and local community and provided for popular councils at the district and county level in the liberal community government law of 7 March 1849. But his successor, Bach, suspended the law a few months later, on 29 October, and thus dug the grave of this most promising institution. The government was afraid—with justice—of a constituent assembly, but it [also] would have nothing to do with a gradual development, stage by stage, of self-government. . . .

Schwarzenberg, as we now know, had only chosen the constitutional renovation in order to have public opinion on his side in the struggle with Prussia for dominance in Germany. He never made any secret of his sincerest detestation of the "manure constitution" which he produced in March 1849. But even this "apparent constitutionalism" produced reservations in the immediate entourage of the emperor. In February 1850 people were already talking about the weakening of Schwarzenberg's position. . . . The hand of God showed itself when the brain of Count Stadion, creator of the constitution, collapsed totally.

The gesture was clear. Prince Schwarzenberg believed he dare not

From Viktor Bibl, *Die Tragödie Österreichs* (Leipzig and Vienna, 1937), pp. 244–251. Translated by permission of Dr. Gerhard G. Leitner. This work is an updated and condensed version of his *Der Zerfall Österreichs,* with the sections on Metternich and his era somewhat shortened and a chapter added for the post–World War I period.

overlook it. The diplomatic victory over Prussia offered the welcome vehicle by which, now that the burdensome consideration for public opinion in Germany could [again] be disregarded, the way was open for a return to unlimited absolutism. The leader destined by providence for this fateful march was Baron Kübeck, former president of the court chancellery [*Hofkammer*]. . . . The well-educated, enlightened, once so liberal statesman had been converted since the outbreak of the March Revolution [of 1848] into an unconditional supporter of governmental authority, and the experiences of that stormy year had made him still more conservative. Kübeck was reckoned in the entourage of the emperor as the representative of unlimited personal rule by the monarch and as an opponent of ministerial despotism. He had never withheld his opinion that the constitution was a misfortune for Austria and that it ought not have been necessary for the emperor to promise the people of his empire such a constitution.

At the beginning of December 1850, a short time after the day of [the diplomatic confrontation between Austria and Prussia at] Olmütz, Kübeck, the "Father of Neoabsolutism," was named president of the new Reichsrat, a Governing Council provided for in the March constitution, and in this way the direction was already indicated in which the empire was to go—the elimination of the constitution through a coup. "We've thrown constitutionalism overboard," writes Francis Joseph, visibly relieved, to his mother, "and Austria has henceforth only one master."

Several ministers of character, like Bruck and Schmerling, resigned. The finance minister, Philipp Kraus, followed them, having called attention to the unfortunate effects [of this measure] on the state finances, because the moneyed interests valued parliamentary control. . . . Count Thun, who had religious reservations, was uncertain, as was Bach, but both finally decided to stay. On the last day of the year 1851 Francis Joseph revoked the constitution in all its forms. . . .

As a result of this reversal of direction on the part of the government—as Joseph Redlich cogently remarked—"the whole fate of the empire was tied to a backwards march, leading eventually to the abyss." And in his review of the years of revolution and reform Heinrich Friedjung observes that the moment for setting the empire on a new path through a firmly established constitution, and thereby strengthening it, was never again so favorable. In the new Austria, he said, everything was in the process of becoming, in a condition of crystallization. "At this point in time the atoms had to be put together into firm structures." . . . When in 1867 the division of the empire took place and the thought of a complete separation struck ever deeper roots among the Magyars, then even stiff-necked opponents of parliamentary government had to concede that the revocation of the constitution of 4 March 1849 belonged to those acts which are counted among the greatest political mistakes of history—in the ranks of the "lost opportunities."

The ship of state set all sails for a voyage back into the time of Emperor Francis I and his chancellor Metternich.

The Hapsburg Empire

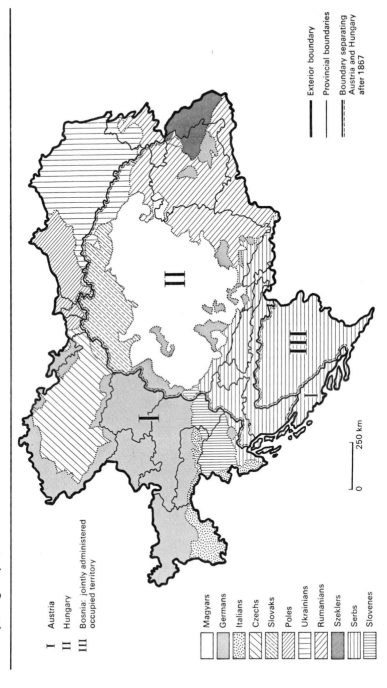

I   Austria
II   Hungary
III Bosnia: jointly administered
      occupied territory

Magyars
Germans
Italians
Czechs
Slovaks
Poles
Ukrainians
Rumanians
Szeklers
Serbs
Slovenes

Exterior boundary
Provincial boundaries
Boundary separating
Austria and Hungary
after 1867

0   250 km

Phase II: Federalism

Just as the Revolution of 1848 had revealed the inability of the old ad hoc imperial authorities to meet the needs of government in the new industrial era, so the defeat of Austria at the hands of France and Piedmont-Sardinia in 1859 brought new weaknesses to light. The Schwarzenberg reforms, the systematization and rationalization of government which remained despite the revocation of the constitution of 1849, were not enough to make the government acceptable in the eyes of its subjects. Some kind of constitutionalism was unavoidable, some participation of some representatives in the government had become a necessity, a condition of survival of the monarchy. This realization on the part of the monarch led to seven years of experimentation with various constitutional forms which had to satisfy two virtually contradictory conditions: to correspond to the existing distribution of political influence, particularly the dominant role hitherto played by the German element, and at the same time appear to offer the other ethnic groups the prospect of realizing some of their aims at some time in the not too distant future. Only a solution embracing some degree of federalism offered any real promise of enduring.

Hugo Hantsch
SCHMERLING AND PARLIAMENTARY GOVERNMENT

The living Austrian historian who stands most directly in the conservative tradition established by Srbik is Hugo Hantsch (b. 1895), priest, professor, first at Graz, then in Vienna. Hantsch, author of a monumental two-volume history of Austria from its beginnings is, though very alive to the power of tradition, not without criticism of the often light-hearted approach of the bureaucracy to Austria's complex problems. In this selection he discusses the Schmerling reforms which followed Austria's defeat in the war of Italian unification.

[After the defeat of the Austrian armies by Napoleon in northern Italy] the critics had an easy time of it citing the damage done by the [neoabsolutist] regime, which had thus unmasked itself. It should have led to power and to greatness, but the result was weakness and disarray. The nation-state idea had triumphed once more over supra-

From Hugo Hantsch, *Die Geschichte Österreichs* (Graz, Vienna, Cologne, 1968), vol. II, pp. 357–365. Translated by permission of Verlag Styria.

national universalism, liberalism over conservatism, and the imperial ambitions of the French emperor, as evidenced by the decisive assistance he gave to the Piedmontese with his troops, served only to reawaken the national spirit in Germany, which, to be sure, had declined to assist Austria, but which also regarded the growing power of Napoleon III with the greatest suspicion. Once more it had been made clear that Prussia, not Austria, was the leading state in Germany, a Prussia which had acquired in Otto von Bismarck a statesman who consciously knew how to use all these advantages for the benefit of his country. Many people in Austria shared the emperor's conviction that only the refusal of the Germanic Confederation [to aid Austria against Napoleon] and the egotism of Prussia were responsible for the defeat and for Austria's loss of the primary position in Italy, and that consequently special effort must be made to strengthen the [Austrian] position in Germany. One means to this end, or rather the precondition for it, should be the loosening up of the absolutist system, an advance to constitutional methods, by which the powerful liberal circles of Germany could be won over. How to find a form, however, which fitted the liberal ideas of the times without breaking up the state structure, which could not dispense with at least some unifying bonds? One must never lose track of this problem, for which no previous pattern existed, if one does not wish to make unfair judgments concerning the constitutional experiments [of this period].

Such basically liberal and generous men as, for example, Baron Bruck did not fail to let the emperor know that the small circle of his most intimate advisors were men of narrow views, mostly military men, who judged things from a military standpoint. Yet more than words convinced the almost thirty-year-old monarch—who since 1854 had been married to Elizabeth, daughter of Duke Max of Bavaria, a lady not wholly unresponsive to liberal ideas—[that] the unfortunate experiences of his first years in power indicated the need for a change. He [therefore] dismissed the once highly influential *general-adjutant* Count Grünne and the police minister Kempen and replaced Dr. [Alexander] Bach with a respected member of the Polish aristocracy, Count Agenor Goluchowski, as head of the Ministry of the Interior. In June 1859 the old Count Clemens Metternich died, convinced to the end of the rightness of his ideas, [thus unburdening the emperor of this uncomfortable advocate of outdated measures]. In a manifesto issued from Laxenburg and dated 15 July 1859 Francis Joseph turned to his people and promised them appropriate improvements in administration and legislation. But how could a compromise be found between the two leading concepts of the day, the one a liberal-centralistic point of view advocating a Reichstag and limited autonomy for the provinces, the other basically federalistic-autonomistic, arguing for the broadest possible scope for the provincial legislatures?

It was decided to latch onto an institution saved from the March constitution, the Reichsrat [imperial council], strengthened by additions up to fifty-nine members, with the archduke Rainer, who was known for his liberal views, at its head. That was, of course, no constitutional device, even less a form of popular representation, but rather a kind of representation by estate, in which the aristocracy played a leading role and attempted to bring its federalistic point of view to bear. Count Anton Szécsen, the old conservative Hungarian magnate, and Count Henry Clam-Martinic, the high noble from Bohemia, really represented the thoughts of this influential group with its essentially class-oriented interests, which they tried to express through the structure of the old historic provinces. Too hastily, with too little careful thought, they put together a report which, to be sure, did not recommend a representative constitution, but rather the return to constitutional conditions [as they had formerly existed].

This report laid the basis for that new constitution which, as the so-called October Diploma, was published on 20 October 1860 and was described in the accompanying manifesto as "a permanent and irrevocable basic law of the state" issued on "the basis of the Pragmatic Sanction and given force through our [the monarch's] unrestricted authority," that is, by grace of a monarch conscious of his absolute power. The manifesto confirmed the essence of the constitution, which "should adjust the demands, legal attitudes, and legal claims of the provinces and the nationalities to the actual requirements of the monarchy, to which the historical consciousness, the existing differences among the kingdoms and provinces, and the needs of their inseparable and unconquerable bonds of unity should equally correspond." Accordingly, the principal weight should rest on the provincial legislatures, which [would] jointly elect one hundred members of the Reichsrat. The latter was authorized to participate in legislating on matters of common interest affecting the provinces (money and credit, customs, trade and transit, evaluation of the budget), while in all other matters the provincial legislatures themselves were called on to "participate" [directly in legislating]. To be sure, the Hungarian legislature was granted more extensive rights than the provincial representations of the other provinces, for it was to receive once again the significance it had enjoyed prior to 1848. Hungary and the Siebenbürgen once more received special representation at the court in Vienna, Magyar became the official language [in Hungary], the *Comitates*[1] were restored to life. The province of the Voivodina was united with Hungary, while the "triple kingdom" (Croatia, Slavonia, Dalmatia) was to retain its own provincial legislature.

Despite extensive decentralization of the administration and despite the participatory right in legislation conceded to the provinces, the absolute central administration still retained overriding importance. The Hungarians remained dissatisfied with this arrangement; they were unprepared to accept direction from Vienna in the interests of the empire. "Historic right," which received official recognition in the October Diploma, looked otherwise to them. But even German liberalism was unable to produce any sympathy for such a "new order," representing anything but a fundamental change, an organic reconstruction of the empire. The impossibility of putting this constitution into effect was immediately clear. The state could not be helped any more by half concessions, which merely embellished absolutism. It must have been a severe trial to the emperor to bring himself to entrust the creation of a new constitutional instrument to that Anton Ritter von Schmerling who had once functioned in Frankfurt [in 1848] as liberal minister. Just for this reason all the hopes of the liberals and especially of the Germans rested with him. One should not forget that the emperor was motivated not merely by concern for internal policy, but that the re-creation of Austria's financial, military, and diplomatic authority was closest to his heart. The reality of momentary diplomatic circumstances was the prime motive for his actions, not any theoretical political idealism.

In Vienna Ritter von Schmerling in cooperation with that knowledgeable Tiroler, Hans von Perthaler, drafted the constitution which remained in force in its basic form until the collapse of the monarchy, thus proving itself, though not without certain sweeping changes, as a sound foundation of real constitutional life. For this reason a more exact description of its contents is justified. First of all, the expression

---

[1] County councils composed of the Magyar nobility and gentry, which were responsible for local government in Hungary.

"February Patent" is not wholly appropriate; for the imperial "Patent" is merely the introduction to the whole complex of laws, which are better described as "February constitution." After the Patent signed by the emperor and the entire cabinet came the "Fundamental State Law" on imperial representation and finally the provincial regulation with the electoral provisions for the provincial legislatures and the Reichsrat.

The whole constitutional structure arises from the sovereign will of the ruler; it is an act of grace of the emperor, which, however, once established, binds him and his successors. In the Patent it was described as the "form and manner" in which the legislative rights granted in the October Diploma to the imperial and provincial representative bodies should be exercised in practice, a not very successful veiling of the failure of the attempted federalistic experiment six months earlier; for the February constitution truly differs, not merely in form, from the October Diploma, it stands on an entirely different political and ideological basis. But it is an imperial constitution, which includes Hungary, Croatia, Slavonia, and the Siebenbürgen.

The representative body of the empire carries the title Reichsrat whereby reference to the sovereign will of the people, as would be the case with Reichstag, is avoided. It consists, after the English pattern, of a House of Lords and a House of Deputies. As hereditary or official members of the [former] house were the following: adult princes of the royal house and the adult representatives of those Austrian noble families to whom Francis Joseph granted the right of an hereditary seat; all archbishops of princely rank; as members for life "outstanding individuals who had won deserving fame in state or church, science or art" and who were appointed by the emperor. The House of Lords represented therefore a very conservative element, an elite of men who stood out through birth or office, merit or intellectual achievement, an effective counterweight against possible future democratic tendencies in the House of Deputies, whose 343 members, divided among the provinces according to a particular formula, were deputed by the provincial legislatures. These latter elect their representatives, however, not as a whole but rather in curias.[2] This indi-

---

[2] Class groupings, such as large property owners, leading merchants, and the like. Thus under the original scheme the major class groupings would be assured of the right to the same representation in the Reichsrat as in the provincial legislatures, but the election would be indirect—the class deputies in the provincial legislature choosing, by class, their

rect election can be replaced by a direct election through the curias of the provinces if the provincial legislature declines to make the selection. What was here provided for as exception and emergency measure became, in the electoral reform of 1873, the rule. At first, however, the physiognomy of the imperial representative body was essentially dependent on the structure of the provincial legislatures.

The provincial legislatures were normally composed of three or four curias, large property holders, cities and chambers of commerce, and rural communities. By large property holders was meant the owners of land recorded in the registry of deeds, that is, land that counted as noble. Thus in this case the suffrage was tied to real property, not to a particular person. In Bohemia, Moravia, and Silesia a distinction was made among high aristocratic, entailed, and ordinary freehold property, by which the former enjoyed a certain political preference. In the Vorarlberg, where no landed property of this type existed, this curia was missing, so that in that province a democratic point of view could develop somewhat more readily, which in any case corresponded to the self-conscious spirit of the inhabitants of this tiny land. In the Tirol, where no registry of deeds existed, landed property had to belong either to the aristocracy or the church in order to enjoy political rights. The possessors of large estates who already enjoyed considerable influence as a result of their social and economic position were [thus] granted political rights which assured them of extraordinary authority in relation to their very limited numbers, a state of affairs which can only be regarded as a survival of their power position in the old class society.

Both in the [municipal] corporations and in the rural communities suffrage depended on the possession of some property, that paid at least 10 *gulden* direct taxes, which gave to the middle-class element—and in communities of mixed nationalities, the German element—exceptional weight. The October Diploma has been described as a "coup of the high aristocracy against the central bureaucracy." In Schmerling's system, on the other hand, the centralistic German bureaucracy allies itself with the moderate liberalism of the overwhelmingly German upper middle class of the empire. One cannot speak of a democratic suffrage; for the greatest part of the populace is excluded from participation in an active political life. This, how-

own representative for the Reichsrat. After 1873 each class, or curia, elected its Reichsrat representative directly, not indirectly as in the original scheme.

ever, was not exclusively Austrian, for the road to democracy in Europe passed [everywhere] through a period of middle-class institutions. The English constitution of that period could not be described as democratic either.

In Austria such a temporary solution appeared to be particularly justified because the cultural and educational level of the different classes of the populace and of the nationalities, and consequently political understanding, was so very uneven. The liberal Leopold von Hasner undoubtedly expressed the opinion of many when he said that one could not confine Austria in the straitjacket of mere numbers, "since by this method national majorities would be created which, bearing no relation to quality, would deliver whole national groups over to a hopeless status of eternal minority, in which observation he clearly was thinking first and foremost of the Bohemian situation, where a culturally and economically poorer majority of Czech peasants faced a better educated and more prosperous German minority which declined to give up the position it had acquired by its industry [and frugality]. Here, just as in Galicia, it was a question not merely of a social but also of a difficult national problem of decisive importance for the development of the monarchy. With the cultural unfolding of the rising Czech nation this unhappy relationship of political forces became an acute crisis, even more than in Galicia, where a dominant aristocratic and middle-class Polish populace faced a Ruthenian peasantry without political rights, which contended [however] for social freedom.

The electoral system, which in Bohemia favored the German element, in Galicia the Polish, resulted for example in the Bohemian provincial legislature composed of 241 members, [in a situation in] which 5 persons sat as individuals, 70 as large property holders, 15 as representatives of the chambers of commerce, and 72 of the cities, while only 79 represented the rural communities. In the cities 1 deputy represented 11,666 inhabitants, in the rural communities 49,081. According to a calculation of Francis Palacký, which should, however, be used with caution, Prague with a population of 145,000 inhabitants had 10 deputies, Reichenberg with 19,000 inhabitants 3. The seats of the chambers of commerce, as a result of the dominance of the Germans in industry, fell practically speaking to the German element. Thus the attitude of the large property owners was decisive in Bohemia, they could decide the majority. It is to be noted, however, that the large property owners, although a curia, were [in Bohemia] no party; they were split into those having a liberal, centralistic frame of mind and those advocating a conservative federalism. The first group was represented by Prince Carlos Auersperg, "the first cavalier of the empire," the second by Prince Carl Schwarzenberg and the counts Leo Thun and Henry Clam-Martinic. This internal division [within the group of large property holders] was to be of uncommon significance.

The February constitution differentiated between an "enlarged Reichsrat" whose sphere of authority embraced matters affecting all the kingdoms and lands or provinces of the empire and a "smaller Reichsrat" to which the representatives of lands of the Hungarian crown did not belong, so that a sort of precursor of the dualistic structure emerged here. Among the common matters of the whole empire were the following: army, currency and credit, customs and trade, the imperial budget and control of financial measures, loans and governmental properties, taxes and dues, as well as international treaties. Constitutional handling of these matters presupposed a common Reichsrat, which, however, never existed, since the Hungarians never appeared. In such a case the cabinet was authorized to act independently, but with the obligation to report to the next Reichsrat. Practically speaking this proviso handed over to the emperor full power in all common imperial matters, to which foreign policy naturally belonged. That was certainly not the proper intent of a constitution, and it is understandable that the narrower Reichsrat attempted so far as possible to extend its competence, especially in the financial questions which were for that representative group so particularly important, while the crown endeavored as far as possible to curb the independence of this Reichsrat. The frequent, very bitter discussions over authority contributed substantially to making the work of the Reichsrat, in which a number of extremely competent men sat, relatively ineffective and to creating between government and imperial representation a fateful division. Emperor Francis Joseph had not yet advanced so far as to adapt himself honestly and without reservation to constitutional methods.

The Reichsrat was, to be sure, not merely an advisory body, but also possessed the right of initiating legislation; for a bill to become law, however, it required not merely the approval of the majority of both houses but also the assent of the crown. The power of the crown also made itself felt through the appointment of the ministers by the emperor, for they were solely responsible to him, as well through naming the presidents and vice-presidents of the Reichsrat, the selection of the chief administrators of the provinces and their deputies who presided over the provincial legislatures, and the right which the emperor claimed of calling the imperial parliament as well as the provincial legislatures into session, of adjourning and of dissolving them.

The old Reichsrat of the March constitution was to some extent continued in the bureaucratic-centralistic state council [*Staatsrat*], which possessed the not unimportant right of commenting on bills approved by the Reichsrat before they were laid before the emperor for his signature.

From the internal and external structure of the Reichsrat, and especially of the House of Deputies, it must be concluded that it possessed no independent political authority; for its scope was restricted by so many limitations that the government could easily circumvent it altogether. The provincial legislatures could not function as much more than cultural institutions.

The emperor was not trying to suppress the historic rights of the provinces, but square in the center of his thinking was the unity of the empire, which alone could insure the power position of his monarchy in Europe. This was the motive underlying all attempts to bring imperial concepts and local autonomy into some kind of harmony, to uphold the basis of the Pragmatic Sanction, the indivisibility [of the empire]. Yet like all earlier attempts this too failed because Hungary, the country that was central to the problem and whose inclusion in the empire was really the main objective of all these efforts, persistently refused to recognize [the existence of] the empire. . . .

The constitutionalism of the February Patent was from the beginning weak, for not only the Hungarians rejected the constitution. The Croats did not appear [in the Reichsrat] because the promise to create [a separate] triple kingdom (Croatia, Slavonia, Dalmatia) was not fulfilled. Moreover the Croats wanted no part of centralism. Deep unrest spread among this people, which could pride itself on the fact that it had saved the throne for the emperor [in 1848]. Undeniably, the Poles came to the first meeting, but only to present a protest. Their attention was wholly monopolized by the uprising of their compatriots against the czar, an uprising which aroused as much sympathy in liberal circles as concern in conservative governmental. The Czechs also protested against centralism in concert with their noble delegates and then, annoyed at the destruction of their national and constitutional hopes, turned their backs on the parliament in Vienna.

Finally, the Tiroleans also raised their voices, and their leader, the eloquent and fiery priest Joseph Greuter, emphasized that they would never enter the central parliament, the "slaughter-house of our independence," "except under firm guarantees against the bureaucratic, absolutistic aggression of liberalism towards the inherited customs and laws of our forefathers." When the liberal deputy Mühlfeld made an over-hasty proposal for civil marriage and the elimination of the concordat, thus prematurely revealing the antireligious tendencies of liberalism, the newspaper *Vaterland,* closely bound to clerical and aristocratic circles, took up the battle [against liberalism], a battle which continued for half a century, a fight against dechristianization of public life, which the paper regarded as a serious danger to the maintenance of the priceless cultural inheritance of the populace. In the year 1864 a liberal deputy believed he could assure a party friend: "We would surrender ourselves to a great deception, if we tried to believe that the populace itself is at all sympathetic towards the new era." . . .

Julius Miskolczy

THE UNRECONCILED HUNGARIANS

All effort at reforming the government of the Austrian Empire had to come to grips, sooner or later, with the special, privileged position claimed by Hungary. The Hungarians had carried their rejection of imperial unity farthest in 1848, and their intransigeance required the intervention of the czarist armies to suppress the republic proclaimed by Louis Kossuth and his associates. Hungary lost its traditional liberties—its own parliament, a separate coronation of the reigning Habsburg on the basis of a coronation oath, and extensive tax privileges—after 1849. The Hungarian Julius Miskolczy, from 1935 to 1949 professor of history at the university in Budapest, since then honorary professor at the university in Vienna, reveals how this repressive policy left the Hungarians bitter and unreconciled.

At this point in 1859, in the light of the Italian defeat, the men in Vienna were compelled at last to see that the regime was not on sound footings. Not only the Hungarian conservatives recommended return to legality for the future; the new ministers as well, such as Rechberg and Hübner, spoke of the sins of the past regime and recommended reconciliation. There were large demonstrations in Pest; at the same time the Hungarian members of the strengthened Reichsrat, without exception people of great governmental experience and unshakable loyalty to the dynasty and to the whole monarchy, demanded the restoration of historic rights. After thoroughgoing consultations the monarch allowed himself to be convinced of the need to found the monarchy on a basis of the historical-political individualities but rejected out of hand the thought of dualism.

The last negotiations before the issuance of the October Diploma shed light on many problems of Austrian politics. Reference was made to the fact that Austria, in its foreign policy a defender of historic rights, could scarcely sacrifice these in its internal policy; that every institution of the monarchy [which was] based on the principle of language would signify capitulation to a revolutionary principle; that the true unity of the empire rested on the Pragmatic Sanction; and that a change in the form of the union could only be carried through in agreement with the law. That was the final rejection of the previous

From Julius Miskolczy, *Ungarn in der Habsburger Monarchie* (Vienna and Munich, 1959), pp. 123–129. Translated by permission of Herold Druck–u. Verlagsgesellschaft M.b.H.

regime with its artificial structure and its absolutism. The fundamental idea of reconciliation—and of the later Compromise—was voiced however by Georg Mailáth, the chief judge of Hungary: the interests of Austria and Hungary are constantly identical [he said] because the focal point of Hungary can never lie outside the empire. This recognition was enlarged by the reflection that the strength and power of Hungary were every bit as necessary for the monarchy as the resources of Austria for Hungary: separation would bring great harm to both.

These wise and loyal acknowledgments represented a milestone in the structural history of the Habsburg monarchy. The best Hungarians never ceased to repeat them to their countrymen. After the experiences of the preceding years the conservatives hoped, with the help of these basic truths of Hungarian policy, to win over the public opinion of their land. What they offered, however, the October Diploma, proved not very tempting, particularly in the light of the constitutional expectations. Without doubt the Diploma, with all its not very clear formulations, signified great progress on the road to a constitutional system, but it sacrificed [the claims of] 1848 and thus did not correspond to the demands of historic right. Certain principles, as for example the creation or preservation of a Reichsrat with authority for the whole empire; the reservation of all essential matters of the administration for the determination by law authorized by the Reichsrat, for example the currency, money, and credit, the customs duties, commercial matters, currency issue, post, telegraph and railroad operation, the status of compulsory military service recruits, the introduction of new taxes and loans, the national debt, etc., left for the *Landtage* [provincial legislatures], including the Hungarian Reichstag, an extremely limited sphere of activity.

As the foregoing makes clear, Hungary had had a part of the abovementioned rights since time immemorial, or she had fought unceasingly for them, until 1848 brought autarchy. Only conservatives alien to the public opinion of their own country could dream that Hungary would accept such a degree of centralization with its sacrifice of ancient rights. Had the government advanced such a proposal in the fall of 1849, there would have been some prospect of its acceptance; the public statements of 1859 and 1860 made the acceptance of the Diploma from the beginning illusory. Deák said as much in his second Address draft, a half a year later; the extension of the Diploma to Hungary could not be accepted [he said] and could not [even] serve, in the deliberations of the Hungarian Reichstag, as a basis [for discussion]. The reestablishment of the old Hungarian institutions as well as the organs of autonomous administration was certainly accepted with satisfaction, still in the *Comitates* [county councils] the prevailing attitude about the fate of this step by the government was never in doubt. This attitude was not modified by essential national concessions like the reintroduction of Hungarian as a governmental language. The famous publicist Baron S. Kemény rightly praised the men of the October Diploma, yet at the same time he confirmed that they had once again committed the old mistakes, misunderstanding the true opinion of the land; [for] no nation could sacrifice the ideas for which it had made a great revolution, the whole Hungarian nation regarded 1848 as a law, [and the repression of] 1849 on the other hand as an imposed dictatorial measure. One could not have characterized the situation any more clearly.

Francis Joseph did not possess the statesmanlike genius of his great-grandfather, Leopold II. He did not understand how far he could and should go with concessions in order to conclude an acceptable compromise with the Hungarians. Certainly he took one step forwards, only to take immediately thereafter another backwards. The February Patent has to be regarded as such a backwards step, seen from the standpoint of the settlement of the question of states' rights. Perthaler's notion, to set liberal constitutionalism against the national idea, was hardly likely to win friends among the Hungarian public. In principle the two constitutional points of view were opposed to one another, without the possibility of compromise: the Hungarian, which clung to the principle of absolute legitimacy and continuity of right, which held the constitutionally created laws of 1848 as unconditionally valid; and the point of view of the government, which did not recognize their validity and, seen from the standpoint of application, was only prepared to recognize so much of Hungarian states' rights as the monarch, in his generosity, considered it appropriate to give back to the land. Rejection of the laws of 1848 meant, in fact, rejection of the whole of Hungarian states' rights.

The February Patent declared that the Reichsrat was set up for the representation of the empire and allowed Hungary 85 representatives out of a total of 343. It thus pushed the kingdom into the status of a hopeless minority and exceeded the Diploma of 20 October 1860 in its limitations on Hungary's constitutional rights. The Reichsrat of the Diploma could, *mutatis mutandis,* be regarded as an enlarged and modernized successor of the former *Staatsrat* [advisory council] which, in the Hungarian constitution, could be recognized as an advisory body to the monarch; the Patent, however, created a parliament with a great number of members and with two houses. Regarded from the Hungarian standpoint, the Patent was also unacceptable because Hungary, according to the terms of the law, could scarcely ever hope to win over the two-thirds majority of both houses necessary for a constitutional amendment. Acceptance would have meant final rejection of dualism. The Diploma, the work of Hungarian statesmen, had represented the principle of autonomy, the Patent that of centralization. A national parliament was created by Schmerling which left for the *Landtage* only a shadow existence, less than the Diploma. No wonder the Hungarian press unanimously rejected the Patent and that the *Comitates,* playing themselves up as protectors of constitutionality, decisively rejected its validity. No more unlucky preliminary for the soon-to-convene Reichstag of Hungary could be found: in the entire country there was only one slogan, 1848, the continuity of right.

Deák's[1] two proposals for the Address [to the monarch] as well as his speech on the history of the whole monarchy have made the [Hungarian] Reichstag of 1861 famous. He rejected above all the idea of an imposed constitution, of any kind of imposition at all; and demanded the restoration of the old constitution which grew out of the life of the nation. That was a decided rejection of Schmerling's Address and of the Hungarian conservatives. He described the recreation of the legal foundation and the independence of the kingdom as the basis for a constitutional government and attempted to show that the October Diploma limited the constitution of Hungary, making Hungary [nothing more than] an Austrian province, whereby it violated the basic law of the monarchy, the Pragmatic Sanction.[2] This last was described by Deák as a fundamental treaty that could not be unilaterally altered. He had found in this basic law and in other Hungarian laws, he declared, the definition of the tie between Hungary and the Austrian crown lands: this tie exists in the identity of the person of the

[1] Francis Deák (1803–1876), leader of the moderate liberals in the Hungarian legislature, co-negotiator with Baron Andrassý of the Compromise of 1867.
[2] Pragmatic Sanction, negotiated by Charles VI in 1713, secured the succession in Hungary to his daughter, Maria Theresa, in return, for a guarantee in perpetuity of Hungary's constitutional prerogatives.

monarch, in the personal union, whereas of a real union there is no trace in the Hungarian laws; Hungary had concluded a treaty with the dynasty and not with the crown lands, though it was prepared to negotiate with the latter over common interests if need should arise, as independent land with independent land, and to conclude agreements, but rejected all drives directed at fusion, did not want to take part in the Reichsrat or in any other imperial representation or recognize its authority over the affairs of Hungary. . . .

The situation proved to be not yet ripe for reconciliation. On the one hand, Deák could only manage in the [Hungarian] Reichstag to push through a form of the Address acceptable to the monarch, instead of a resolution designed to show that the Reichstag regarded Francis Joseph as the illegitimate, if actual, master of Hungary. In the matter of the Reichstag, the deputies were at one with Deák's instransigeance; moreover, Perthaler and Schmerling represented points of view which the Hungarians, even the conservatives, could hardly accept. Once again the royal answer advanced the principle of the real union and rejected any recognition of the laws of 1848; as a condition for further negotiations [the central government] demanded the reevaluation of the laws of 1848 in a manner corresponding to the interests of the entire monarchy. The conservatives were dismissed by the monarch after their unsuccessful attempt [to mediate].

Schmerling's policy could well be [regarded as] in many respects grounded on the nationality question. The Rumanians took a decided stand against the union of Siebenbürgen with Hungary, and the Croatian *Landtag* renewed the demands of 1848, as for instance the complete independence of the Croatian state, a tie with the mother country [solely] on the basis of a personal union, and further the possession of the Istrian peninsula and the harbor of Fiume, but left open the possibility of negotiation. The Slovaks demanded an autonomous area for themselves. Despite the disappointments the nationalities had had to suffer during the Bach era, the government believed itself able to count on their loyalty. But that still offered no satisfactory substitute for the unanimous rejection of the Schmerling proposal in the Hungarian Reichstag.

The second Address of the Reichstag was also Deák's work and it was in no way inferior to the first in clarity, logic, and decisiveness. It rejected the supposition that the nation would accept an imperial Diploma and a Patent in place of its laws, demanded the legislative power for the whole legislative body, demanded for the Reichstag the right of determining the position of recruits and of fixing the taxes. Only in foreign affairs was it prepared to recognize the exclusive authority of the monarch; otherwise it rejected the claim for full royal powers. What the Address had to say over joint matters is significant: the country remained true to the terms of the Pragmatic Sanction in the sense that, besides this basic law, no other tie existed between the identity of the monarch and the inseparable and indivisible property which rested on that commitment. But it declared that as Hungary did not want to endanger the existence and the Great Power status of the monarchy, which the laws of 1848 did not do, it was even prepared, above and beyond its obligations, to assist the crown lands in carrying the heavy burden [of the debt], so that the welfare of the crown lands and of Hungary would not collapse under its weight. The conclusion was still, however, the insistence that Hungary stood firm on the Pragmatic Sanction, did not accept the October Diploma and February Patent as a basis for the negotiations in the Reichstag, did not send deputies to the Reichsrat [in Vienna], did not give up the right to decide on taxes and the military draft in the Reichstag. It was also mentioned [in the Address] that the Committee for Nationality Questions under the guiding influence of Baron Eötvös had established certain ground rules for the solution of this thorny question, among others the principle of a political nation and the equality of the nationalities inhabiting the land.

Francis Joseph closed the Reichstag; the reconciliation attempt had failed. There is no doubt that the work of the Compromise could have been completed in 1861, if the firm determination to do so had been present. Since Villafranca everyone on both sides had had the feeling that the situation could not be maintained, that the interest of the monarchy urgently required a compromise.

Edvard Beneš

THE UNRECONCILED CZECHS

Edvard Beneš (1884–1948), leader of the Czech liberals, later premier and finally president of the Czechoslovak Republic, analyzed the Czech reaction to Schmerling's plans for imperial constitutional reform in his doctoral dissertation at the University of Dijon in France. He shows very clearly how, in the case of the Czechs as of the Hungarians, the claims of 1848 remained the national program, requiring a degree of local autonomy inconsistent with the view of imperial unity prevailing among the ministers and the bureaucracy in Vienna.

Learning from experience, the Czechs ceased to think of a federation of the nationalities. Palacký, in his *The Idea of the Austrian State,* expressed himself plainly in favor of a federalist program, but it was a federation of lands, of provinces, which he demanded. They wanted a federal Austria composed of autonomous lands, and they defended this program against the German centralists in the Bohemian Diet and in the Reichsrat in Vienna. Thus the Czechs revived the political program which they had accepted at the time of the Kremsier constitution in 1848. They frankly continued in their federalist program, laying aside for the moment the historical program.

The October Diploma, published by the government on 24 October 1860, gave the Czechs a certain satisfaction. It even aroused general enthusiasm among them for its federal and liberal provisions. It has [since] become the point of departure for all the national claims of the Czechs. Since then the sole object of the Czechs has been its actual realization. To be sure, the Czechs allowed themselves some illusions as to its real importance. But Schmerling's scandalous application of it in the February Patent disappointed them at the time and irritated them. The February constitution, decreed by the February Patent, had in it almost nothing of the tendencies of the Diploma. Centralism and a considerable dose of absolutism were, on the contrary, its [the Patent's] leading characteristics.

The Czech deputies to the [Bohemian] Diet formulated their reservations against the Patent. Nonetheless, after some hesitation, they

From Edvard Beneš, *Le Problème Autrichien et la Question Tchèque* (Paris, 1908), pp. 169–177. Translated by permission of Librairie Sociale et Economique.

also entered the central parliament established by the February constitution, but a part of their delegation expressed anew its reservations. Although open adversaries of the new centralism consecrated
by the February constitution, they believed it necessary to enter the
Schmerling parliament and to defend their rights there. To be sure,
they did so not without hesitation, some resistance, and some internal
struggles [among the Czech deputies].

In Vienna the Czechs protested against the application of the October Diploma in the February Patent and formulated their federalist
program, or rather their program of autonomous centralism, in a
declaration in which they stated further: "We want an Austria in which
all the countries and all the peoples are equal in law, where all have
the same relationship to the central government, where all are equally
and justly represented. Austria can never be a German state, nor a
Hungarian, nor a Slav, only uniquely Austrian, with equal rights for all
the peoples, federated in public life, in the representative system, in
legislation, and in administration."

In his celebrated study, *The Idea of the Austrian State,* Palacký
formulated precisely the national program of the Czechs. He confirms
that the idea of the right of nationalities suffered a certain eclipse in
Austria after 1848, especially since the Eötvös doctrine of politico-
historical individualities was generally adopted. He renounced his idea
of reorganizing Austria on the basis of a federation of nations and
accepted the theory of the politico-historical individualities. Nonetheless it is the federation of nations which he proclaimed as the national
program. He was prepared to concede to the central power the affairs
of the dynasty, foreign affairs, war, common finances, and domestic
and foreign trade. On the other hand, the administration of the land,
instruction, courts, and other matters would be the province of the
individual lands. The very small lands could be united into larger
groups. Each group would have its judges, its administration, its
chancellor or minister to the central government. The central parliament would consist of delegations from the Diets [provincial legis-
latures], it would not meet regularly, but on specific occasions, according to need, varying from one situation to another, ad hoc. Indirect taxes would be the province of the parliament, direct taxes would
belong to the Diets. In his proposal Palacký reveals himself as the
resolute opponent of dualism.

Palacký published his *Idea* in 1865. Despite the proven deceptions [of the ministry] at the time the Diploma went into force, the Czechs courageously continued their federalist policy. The parliament [Reichsrat] of Schmerling's Patent remained a torso, however, for Hungary—with the exception of Transylvania—never sent any delegates. [As a result] the German centralists had a majority in the Reichsrat and the Slav advocates of autonomy were reduced to impotence. It is therefore very understandable that they adopted the same position as the Magyars and the Croats: on 17 June 1863 the Czech delegates quit the Reichsrat and soon afterwards the delegates from Moravia followed their example. It was the beginning of the Czechs' passive policy which for various reasons was continued until 1879 and which had fatal consequences for the Czechs, especially since they continued this tactic under quite different conditions unfavorable to passive resistance.

In sum, during the political struggles of 1867, up to the conclusion of the Austro-Hungarian compromise, the Czechs remained faithful to their program of 1848 and Austrian federation. They defended it with tenacity—even after having quit the parliament of 1863—against the absolutist government, against the centralist Germans, and against the Magyar separatists. They succumbed to the coalition of these three powers. And it was precisely this defeat which constrained them later to change their program and their tactics.

One can also see that all the political efforts of the Czechs were in complete contradiction to the foreign policy of the government. The foreign policy of the dynasty was entirely opposed to the federalist tendencies of the Slavs. While the Czechs elaborated their program of a federal Austria, the government, always having its foreign plans in mind, pursued its centralist German policy, and when this collided with the invincible resistance of the Magyars, [the government], pushed by foreign developments, by the menacing attitude of Prussia in Germany, and finally exhausted by the war, abandoned Hungary to the Magyars in order to assure Austria to the Germans: it changed its centralist policy into a dualist policy.

In effect, when Palacký published his studies on *Austrian Federalism* in 1865, the groundwork for dualism had already been laid. The government had assured its success with the October Diploma, with its maladroitness in the February Patent, by its practice of favoring all the points of view of the Magyars; and the latter, seeing the difficulties of the dynasty abroad, seized the opportunity to attain their end. The passive resistance of Hungary and later of the Czechs made the failure of Schmerling's constitution inevitable. The war with Prussia for primacy in Germany was imminent; the monarchy was being torn apart by its domestic difficulties, and the resistance of the Hungarians was, in case of war, a source of great uneasiness. Schmerling's inability to achieve the conciliation of Hungary and an entente with the Hungarians led to his fall. His successor, Belcredi, abrogated at once the February constitution and began to negotiate with Hungary, to regularize the relations of Austria and the [central] government with that country. Although surrounded by enormous difficulties, the government was not prepared to give up the idea of a central parliament at any price nor to go so far in its concessions to the Magyars [as they demanded]. But during the negotiations the war broke out. Austria, beaten at Sadowa [Königgrätz], exhausted and powerless, capitulated to the Magyars. The new minister Beust succeeded in negotiating an understanding with Deák, and on 30 March 1867 dualism was established.

The efforts of the Magyars found no more resolute adversaries than the Czechs. For the reasons already indicated, the Slavs wanted the federalistic system for the entire monarchy, including, on the same basis, Hungary. The grounds they advanced were serious. In his *Idea* Palacký fought dualism without reservation, and Rieger [Palacký's successor as leader of the Czechs] was no more indulgent toward the Magyar policy. The Czechs, the Poles, and other Slavs protested to the ministry and even to the emperor against Magyar separatism. For the Czechs, the unity of the monarchy was particularly necessary and indispensible.

On the one hand, the Magyars, who were to become in the central parliament the most resolute of autonomists, would have [had] with the Czechs the majority against the German centralists [if true federalism had been established]. The expansion of the German element would thus have been halted. On the other hand, with the support of the Magyars they would have been able to give to the land a much broader autonomy, since only with their support would the true federal Austria be constructed in opposition to the government and the Germans. In fact, in the dualistic monarchy the Slavs of Cisleithania were sacrificed arbitrarily to the artificial majority of the Germans, those of Transleithania to the artificial majority of the Magyars. On both sides it was a disaster for the entire Slav people. In contrast, in a federal monarchy and in a central parliament [of a federal monarchy], the Slavs would have had the majority and thereby the preponderance. Their political future, their development, and their national existence would be assured. Thus the Slavs and the Czechs could not hesitate for a moment in their struggle against dualism.

Thus there was a complete contradiction between the Czech and the Magyar policy. The Magyars knew that they would be the strongest and the freest if they remained alone in Hungary. Hence their entire policy. It is interesting that it was the Czechs and the other Slavs, the most oppressed by the government, who were at this hour as in 1848 the sole loyal defenders of the unity of the monarchy and the sole devotees of Austria, the sole Austrian patriots. But now with the Austro-Hungarian compromise they were once more deceived, their political goal annihilated, their national program reversed. It was necessary to reorient their political efforts completely. They had to limit themselves to Austria alone. The Slavs of Hungary, even the Slovaks, are henceforth for the Czechs practically foreigners. The Austrian problem became very simple. It was reduced almost exclusively to the Czech question. But the other non-German nationalities of Austria, now more developed and better prepared for the struggle, appeared as well on the political scene and the Austrian problem remained as delicate as it was before the Austro-Hungarian compromise.

With the conclusion of the Austro-Hungarian compromise, the constitution of February, suspended in any case two years previously as a result of the difficulties with the Magyars and the complete failure to which it had been subjected, became superfluous. The parliament convoked in 1867 by Beust, which had to adopt the Austro-Hungarian compromise and thus concede its application in Austria, also received the task of giving Cisleithania a new constitution. This task could only be fulfilled by a parliament in which the centralists had the majority over the Slavs, since the federalist Slavs were simultaneously the adversaries of the Compromise and of a centralist constitution. The parliament of Beust, composed of delegates elected under extreme government influence, was able to fulfill this task, especially since the Czechs refused to appear in the Assembly. The Czechs naturally fought bitterly all efforts which would legally consecrate the division [of the country into two independent halves] and which would aggravate the already precarious situation of the Slavs: for this new constitution would only apply to Cisleithania, it would be centralist for Austria alone as the February constitution was centralist for the entire monarchy. It amounted to replacing the old centralism with a Cisleithanian centralism.

The Czechs protested nonetheless against dualism and against the new constitution. They continued their tactic of passive resistance, they abstained from the activities of the Beust parliament where the German centralists were the majority, adopted the Compromise, and voted a new constitution. This constitution signified a certain amelioration in the direction of federalism, but it was always centralist and unitary [in spirit]. The Czechs were unable to accept such a constitution, which had its origin in such a singular situation, which was voted despite all their efforts, and whose adoption signified the voluntary abdication of all their national rights. Their hope of founding a federal Austria crumbled against the desires of the Magyars and the Germans for domination and against the firm determination of the government to create a unitary and centralist Austria. If they [the Czechs] did not want to accept dualism, it was so much the less possible for them to accept the new Cisleithanian centralism.

They continued in their opposition to the German centralists and against the government. But their entire political program of a federal reorganization of the monarchy was based on unrealizable hypotheses after the conclusion of the Compromise; they had necessarily to look for a new goal for their political efforts and a new national program.

Phase III: Dualism

Despite the valiant attempts of a variety of negotiators to forge an acceptable constitutional compromise, the events of the 1860s made it clear that none of the major ethnic elements of the empire was prepared to accept a scheme in which it did not enjoy at least potential, if not actual, supremacy. The Czechs, as the most advanced Slavic element, persisted in seeking a system based essentially on numbers of inhabitants, because the Slavs represented the largest numerical element in the empire. The Hungarians clung to historic rights, because these assured them of supremacy in one-half the empire, even if the price for this supremacy was segregation from the rest of the empire: in effect a kind of semisecession. The remainder of the empire, not being united as the North was in America at the same time, proved unable to stand against this virtual withdrawal. Finally, the Germans, as the principal supporters of and beneficiaries from imperial unity, tried to preserve as much power for the bureaucracy, their bailiwick and the principal imperial cement, as could be salvaged from the pressures for democratization. In the last analysis foreign affairs, the defeat of Austria at the hands of Prussia, provided the immediate impetus for a solution which enshrined in permanent constitutional commitments the particular constellation of political forces prevailing in 1867. Austria became even more than before the product of historic coincidence.

Eduard von Wertheimer

THE COMPROMISE OF 1867: RESTORATION OF MAGYAR RIGHTS

The defeat of Austria at the hands of Prussia in 1866 made a new constitutional settlement imperative in the mind of the emperor. Convinced that the persistent refusal of the Hungarians to cooperate in the government of the empire lay at the heart of Austria's constitutional difficulties, the imperial government determined to seek a settlement with the Hungarians. Primarily the work of a few influential individuals, as Wertheimer clearly shows in his biography of Count Julius Andrássy, the Compromise of 1867 in fact conceded virtually all those rights claimed by the Hungarians in 1847–1848. Yet as Wertheimer (1848–1930), professor on the law faculty of the Royal Academy of Law in Pressburg, shows, this settlement at last made of the Hungarians loyal citizens of the empire.

As long as Belcredi remained in office [as prime minister] and continued to insist on [convening] the extraordinary Reichsrat and on the federalistic plans which were bound up with it, no possibility of a coronation in Hungary existed. But just this was regarded by the emperor as the crowning achievement of the whole search for a compromise. The empress shared his desire; the latter's pro-Hungarian tendencies culminated in the desire to see the relation of the dynasty to this kingdom put on a sound legal basis. When, after the defeat of Königgrätz, Francis Joseph felt himself isolated in the central palace in Vienna and, in one of the most critical moments of his life, dedicated himself to the great issue of the future structure of the monarchy, Elizabeth threw her weight into the scales on Hungary's side. This happened, to be sure, in opposition to Belcredi, who consequently accused her of having used the emotional condition of the emperor "to lend support to the egotistical efforts of the Hungarians, which she had long and fruitlessly patronized." The empress was genuinely concerned, as was often [later] admitted, to establish peace between the Hungarian nation and the crown; she believed that in this way her husband and the monarchy would be strengthened and made more important.

From Eduard von Wertheimer, *Graf Julius Andrássay: Sein Leben und Seine Zeit* (Stuttgart, 1910), vol. I, pp. 270–74, 276, 290, 293, 295–97, 320, 321–22. Translated by permission of Deutsche Verlags-Anstalt G.m.b.H.

Elizabeth, a truly outstanding personality, was born to this mission. Everyone who had the good fortune to know her admired not only her captivating appearance—she was regarded as one of the most beautiful women of Europe—but also her intellectual capabilities, which produced the impression that one encountered in her a princess whose brains were equal to her beauty. She had no inclination toward intrigue and deplored that flattery to which court life all too easily leads, and she remained in most cases true to the tradition of the Vienna court that women do not mix in affairs of state. Her whole being was opposed to such political activities; as she once said, "I have too little respect for politics, and don't think it worthy of interest." If "politicking," which so often wounded the finer sensibilities, was unable to arouse her interest, she compensated for this by dedicating herself even more to the encouragement of culture. Literature attracted her particularly. She found support in the thinkers and poets of world literature which enabled her to meet the unpleasantnesses of life. Only on rare occasions, on such, she once said, as her position required her attention, did she abandon the restriction which she had imposed on herself and turn to politics, for which she had so little respect. For Hungary's sake she was untrue to her principle, and this was her ideal, to play the role of peacemaker. . . .

How did it come about that this princess, native of a land some distance from Hungary—she was the daughter of Duke Max of Bavaria—in whose childish ears the Hungarian tongue had never sounded, was able to work up such enthusiasm for that land? The riddle can only be solved psychologically. When Elizabeth, at the side fo her imperial bridegroom, first entered the court of Vienna, she encountered a basically anti-Hungarian attitude. Everything was still governed by the impression created by the revolution of the Hungarian people against the chains that despotically inclined statesmen had tried to fasten on them. The young queen encountered only the most unfavorable opinions of the inhabitants of the land beyond the Leitha.

[But] as an independent-minded individual who liked to judge everything herself, Elizabeth decided to take a closer look, to decide for herself if the Hungarians were really so terrible as they had been described to her. To her unprejudiced eyes a quite different picture rapidly unfolded. In a short time she developed a warm sympathy for the noble, faithful, open-hearted Hungarian—qualities which harmonized with her own character. The very friendly reception accorded to her and her husband during a trip through Hungary won her over altogether. She had to concede that a people which greeted its ruler, although he had not yet been crowned, in a thoroughly dignified if not enthusiastic fashion, as was the case in 1857, simply could not be composed solely of [born] rebels, but that only the pressure of circumstances could have driven them to revolt. Elizabeth recognized that a strong dynastic feeling was still to be found among the inhabitants of the lands of St. Stephen, and only bad government had been able to deprive the ruler of this valuable treasure in the hearts of his peoples. This recognition led directly to her determination to encourage at the first opportunity, with every means in her power, the reconciliation between king and nation. Thus is to be explained the fact that the difficulties of the Hungarian language did not deter her from learning it. Through the language, which operates like a magical force on men, she hoped to gain access to the innermost nature of the Hungarians, to open up their hearts. In the unanimous opinion of people who knew her well, Elizabeth not merely managed to master the language fully, but spoke it like one born in the land. . . .

Sympathizing as she did so wholly with Hungary, Elizabeth felt herself called upon to restore the bond between throne and nation which had been torn apart by the revolution. Her knowledge of men convinced her that Count Andrássy, one of the leading figures in Hungary, was the most suitable person to effect this peace of reconciliation. That she never had grounds to doubt the wisdom of her choice can be seen in the letters she later sent to Andrássy, in which she addressed him as "dear friend" and signed herself, "your true friend." She invited him to come to see her in order to learn his views about the situation and the best way to get out of the existing difficulties. . . . Despite the pleasant frame of mind which the interview with the empress produced in him, Andrássy did not fail to speak frankly, and to make clear to her that without the speediest possible appointment of a responsible Hungarian ministry, there was no possibility of the re-creation she so ardently desired of good relations between throne and nation. Even then, in October 1866, when according to Elizabeth's own admission the chances for success were very slim, she [nevertheless] promised Andrássy to do everything she could to remove the obstacles in the way of reconciliation. . . .

She found support in the efforts of the men who strengthened the view in the emperor that through reconciliation [he could be recog-

FIGURE 4. Julius Count Andrássy, principal architect of the constitutional Compromise of 1867. *(From the picture archives of the Austrian National Library)*

nized as] king of Hungary and the resulting addition to his authority would enable him to avoid all dangers to throne and empire in the future. This, however, was only to be achieved by the elimination of the constitutional conflicts [in Hungary]. . . . Still shaken by the defeat of Königgrätz and quite discouraged by the failure of the policy suspending [the February constitution], it was merely the natural result of all these circumstances that the emperor now turned away from Belcredi [and gave his confidence to Beust]. Freed of the restricting rivalry of the fallen minister and strengthened by the support of the emperor, the latter made haste to bring the Compromise to a [successful] conclusion. The basis for this lay in the acceptance of the plan of the Committee of Fifty [Hungarian leaders], modified by the [Hungarian Reichstag] Committee of 1867. The outstanding difficulties lay in the revision of the laws of 1848, which now would occur after the appointment of a [responsible] ministry, rather than before as Vienna had formerly demanded.

The emperor had handed over personally to Andrássy the points in which he regarded changes as essential. Among these was paragraph 12 of law III of 1848. The paragraph demanded that the minister-president appointed by the crown present his colleagues to the emperor for confirmation. The crown demanded that these should be presented for nomination, which naturally meant a strengthening of royal authority. Equally, the monarch wanted to see absolute authority over the whole armed forces united in his hands. . . . The ruler therefore wanted the elimination of the special Hungarian military authorities [created during the revolution of 1848]. . . . Deák was opposed to this and during an interview in Vienna urged the emperor to transfer the powers of these *Honved* [national guard] ministries to the minister-president. "I'll think it over," was the sovereign's answer. Deák was very disappointed by this answer. . . . Andrássy promised to try again. . . . The high reputation of Deák with the monarch and the trust he felt toward Andrássy overcame the ruler's reservations against the institution so tainted by revolution. Thus that part [of the Compromise] which concerned defense was cleared up.

But the final regulation of the military structure in general still constituted a delicate question, over which the [negotiations for] the Compromise could have broken down. . . . In December 1866 Beust had already declared that a special constitutional right for Hungary to decide over the calling-up of recruits could not well be combined with the fundamental nature of a unified army. And a few months before, the emperor had said emphatically to Andrássy, "In this question you will find me unyielding." But the count [Andrássy] knew that it would be impossible for him to be generous; a storm of dissatisfaction would have broken out against him in the [Hungarian] Reichstag. . . . The consent to the call-up of recruits was not just an achievement of 1848; the right to this had always existed and had been recognized and confirmed before 1848 in Article 2 of [the laws of] 1840. Thus Andrássy was fully authorized in saying, "The right to consent to the calling up of recruits in the terms of previous Hungarian laws is a right which no

Hungarian Reichstag can give up." As a practical spirit who always tried to mesh real and ideal needs, Andrássy immediately indicated the course which could fulfill the wishes of the military leadership for a strengthened army. He recommended calling for the necessary annual contingent of recruits on the basis of the existing defense system. He did not doubt for a moment that the Reichstag would approve. At the same time, in consequence of the desires of the monarch as commander in chief, immediate steps must be taken to prepare a new law for the organization of the army. In this way, he said, a modification in the *exercise* of the right of approval for calling up recruits could be effected in agreement with the Reichstag. . . .

In the cabinet meeting which took place under the chairmanship of the emperor after final acceptance of the agreement over common matters, the Compromise was perfected . . . [and] achieved a reconciliation between king and nation which could only be compared with that of 1608. Relative to the Pragmatic Sanction of 1722–1723, which enunciated the principle of common defense in general, and in relation to the laws of 1848, which only deal with common matters in a single paragraph, the Compromise of 1867 represents an immense step forward. The law of 1867 makes it very clear that foreign affairs and national defense fall in the realm of common matters. . . .

As can be seen from a letter of Szögyény to Baron Vay, the emperor had been filled with the wish, as early as 1861, to see himself formally crowned [king of Hungary]. A series of severe tests had strengthened the conviction that the crown of Hungary possessed deep significance. This recognition prevented the monarch from committing the error of his ancestor Emperor Joseph II, "the King with the Hat," who regarded the Hungarian crown as a portable possession with which he could do what he liked and who laughed at all those who regarded with deep regret the transfer of this holy treasure from Hungary to the Treasure Room in Vienna as [a symbol of] the destruction of the freedoms of the land. Joseph II had to pay heavily for this mistake and finally had to acknowledge that the Hungarian crown was more than a display item for the treasure chamber, only there to decorate his exterior.

According to the prevailing view the crown of St. Stephen is the fount of all political authority and every right in Hungary. The power of the state is rooted in it. Through the act of crowning the sovereign, rights of the crown are transferred to the ruler, but always with the provision that the king, for his part, recognizes the constitutional rights of the nation by oath and by formal document (*diploma inaugurale*). If one bears in mind the authority granted to the crown, authority which is deeply rooted in the consciousness of the Hungarian nation and which continues to function as an operative force, one can readily see the importance of the act of crowning. It is not, as in other lands, merely a colorful ceremony, but rather, viewed constitutionally, a necessary precondition for the constitutional exercise of royal power. The crowning cannot, however, take place with any crown, but only with the thousand-year-old Stephen's crown, the so-called holy crown. . . .

The peaceful and untroubled course [of the coronation] on 8 June [1867] was very satisfying. The capital of Hungary had not known, at any time in the past, a more decorative and significant celebration than this coronation—a celebration which recognized the re-creation of the constitution and of national independence. Surrounded by the ecclesiastical and secular pride of the nation, which appeared in all its ceremonial finery, the coronation was performed according to the ancient practice, embracing several separate acts. The most dramatic moment occurred as Count Andrássy, in his capacity as representative of the court chamberlain, stepped forward in the middle of the nave of Michael's Church and with the help of the primate, Simor, placed the crown on the anointed head of the monarch. According to the ancient custom he then proclaimed: "The king is crowned, long live the king!"—a joyous cry, to which the crowd present for the ceremony replied with three enthusiastic cheers. Then followed the anointing and the crowning of Elizabeth, who, in all the fullness of youth, enchanted the entire world with her charm and beauty. The coronation oath of the king to the constitution followed in ceremonial fashion in the open air on the Rectory Square in Pest. No less deep an impression was made when Francis Joseph sprang up onto the coronation mound in the present Francis Joseph Square in Pest to deliver the four strokes with the sword by which he signified that he would defend the land against all enemies, from whatever point of the compass they might come. The final act consisted of the state dinner in the Ofen Castle, during which the table of the royal pair was shared only by the primate of Hungary, the archbishop of Kolocsa, the papal nuncio and Graf Andrássy as representative of the court chamberlain. . . .

Public opinion in Austria-Hungary had good reason to be fully satisfied that a "Ministry of Citizens" now conducted Austria-Hungary's state affairs. In Austria, however, there was no sign of the joy which was everywhere evident in Hungary over the beginning of the new constitutional era. . . . In order to understand the oppostition to the new constitutional structure of the monarchy and its unpopularity in the Austrian part of the empire, one has to imagine oneself in the frame of mind of that generation of Austrians. It was hard for the Austrians to accustom themselves to thinking of Hungary, which hitherto had been if not de jure then certainly de facto a mere province, as now, with one stroke, turned into an equal partner. It cost the statesmen of Austria a great deal of self-control to sacrifice the power which in fact Austria had exercised for years in Hungary. Just as with the dissolution of the old Holy Roman Empire in 1806 Vienna was to some degree decapitated, so now the capital had once more to lose some of its former significance. It was a bitter blow for the Austrian ministers to recognize that they had cooperated in an act by which the old imperial city ceased to be the one and only center of the monarchy, that it had to share this role from now on with the Hungarian capital. . . .

But whoever, to use an expression of the younger Andràssy, regards the results of the Compromise from the standpoint of the power interests of the monarchy must confess that the work of Deák and Andrássy has had the most favorable consequences. After the disaster of 1866, which reduced Austria's importance to the lowest level, almost eliminated her from the ranks of the Great Powers, the new monarchy, converted into a dualistic political body, raised itself to unanticipated levels of civilization and power. It acquired once again its proper place in the circle of European powers, a place which Andrássy always wanted it to reacquire. The strengthened Hungary, led by a statesman like Count Andrássy, could no longer be an enemy of that monarchy within whose bounds it now found room for its own development. No enemy of Austria-Hungary could now hope, as in the years between 1850 and 1866, for the help of the Hungarians in the destruction of the monarchy. The days were past when Kossuth, with the expectation of an enthusiastic response, could preach war against the House of Habsburg. Whenever occasional revolutionary signs emerged, the energetic national government was able to suppress them immediately, without serious opposition, rather with the support of the country itself. The idea of revolution had lost so much of its attraction that a leading *Honved* general, who had risked his life for his father-land in many a hot battle, turned his back on it and became instead an enthusiastic admirer of the constitutionality recreated by Deák and Andrássy. This *Honved* general was Klapka, who, still in exile, wrote to Count Andrássy on 20 June 1867: "I see in this new development, so desired by Providence, the beginning of a new and happy era for our people and the first step in the fulfillment of its task in eastern Europe."

In this respect Klapka had guessed the secretly held views of the Hungarian minister-president [Andrássy], who saw the future political development of the monarchy, not, like earlier Austrian ministers, in intervening in the affairs of western Europe. Andrássy wanted to place the power of the monarchy, newly strengthened by the reconciliation with Hungary, in the service of a policy which assured Austria-Hungary [decisive] influence on all developments in the east [of Europe]. Such a statesmanlike view of the mission of the monarchy must offer it new paths for unfolding its powers and gradually weave the bond of trust that later came into being between Bismarck and Andrássy and reached its highest point in the conclusion of the German-Austrian alliance. But the emperor and king, Francis Joseph I, provided vital support for Andrássy's efforts. Fully aware of his historic calling, which consisted in maintaining the unity of the monarchy and its position as a Great Power, Francis Joseph finally realized, even if only after many severe tests, that this goal could be more easily reached with the aid of the just founded dualistic monarchy than with that of a centralized Austria as conceived by Bach and Schmerling.

Hugo Hantsch

THE COMPROMISE OF 1867: SURRENDER OF THE SLAVS

The Compromise of 1867, though satisfactory to the Hungarians, was bought at the cost of alienating many other elements in the empire, not least the Czechs, who felt themselves entitled to equal consideration. Yet, Hantsch argues, despite the impasse at the center of the empire, promising initiatives did occur at the extremities, for example, in the Bukovina.

After the public announcement of the Compromise [of 1867], the demonstrations of Czech national consciousness followed one another speedily and incisively. The high point of these official pronouncements occurred on 22 August 1868 when eighty-one Czech deputies handed the Bohemian *Landtag* a declaration in which they documented their reasons for not participating in the Reichsrat.

This official publication, whose compelling phraseology and masterly construction corresponded to its importance, presented all the arguments of Bohemian states' rights, as they are called. It denied the legality of the laws of the Reichsrat and demanded as a basis for the solution of the constitutional problem an "Agreement between the most honorable King and the political-historical Bohemian nation as justly and properly represented," accepted as such a representation only one "which rests on an electoral system by which the equality of both nationalities of our fatherland is carried out through an equal application of the same principles," and expressed the wish "to conclude an agreement with our German fellow citizens regarding such institutions, which could prevent the restriction [of the rights] of one or the other of the nationalities of the land by means of the mere power of a majority." It's clear enough: it wasn't the compromise with Hungary in itself that so wounded the national feeling of the Czechs, but that this compromise was concluded only with Hungary and not also with the Czechs, who believed themselves to have an equally incontestible and valid right to their special political status. To be

From Hugo Hantsch, *Die Nationalitätenfrage im alten Österreich: Das Problem der konstruktiven Reichsgestaltung* (Vienna, 1953), pp. 56–61, 62–64. Translated by permission of Herold Druck–und Verlagsgesellschaft m.b.H.

sure, Bohemian states' rights did not stand on as firm a footing as did the Hungarian. Not only was the German population [of Bohemia] wholly unconvinced of them, even the Moravian *Landtag* let it be known that "the country [*Markgrafschaft*] is a land wholly independent of Bohemia, which knows no other fundamental law than the present state and imperial constitution and has, since 1620, never sent delegates to a *Landtag* in Prague, and even before then never without the specific reservation that the conclusions reached there [in Prague] must first be ratified in Brünn; Moravia stands by the *Landtag*'s Resolution of 14 April 1848, which rejects all connection with Bohemia." The Silesian *Landtag* declared its independence in equally decisive terms, and even the Bohemian *Landtag,* where the Germans still possessed the majority, rejected the Czechs' Declaration. With Czech public opinion, however, the Declaration acted as a stimulant for all the national passions.

Once again it was a European development which brought the Czechs of Bohemia nearer to the fulfillment of their wishes. The foundation of the German Empire was a victory of nationalism and at the same time signified the crushing of all hopes of the emperor, the government, and the German [population of the empire] of a certain backing among the south German states. What was begun in 1866, the isolation of Austria-Hungary, was now completed. This demanded the development of a state concept for Austria itself, based on its own position and resources. Just as Emperor Francis Joseph gave way to the wishes of the Hungarians after 1866, he was now prepared to respond to the wishes of the Czechs in substantial measure and once more to alter the structure of the empire according to their desires. Forty years old, he still possessed the adaptability to adjust to the pressures of the times. Count Karl Sigmund Hohenwart, who had served in the internal administration and had previously been leader of the committee of the nobility in Fiume, then director of the chancellery office [*Statthalterei-Abteilung*] in Trent, president of [the administration of] the province in Laibach, and finally administrative chief [*Statthalter*] of *Oberösterreich,* received the task of directing this project. He provided himself with an assistant in the person of the minister of commerce and trade, Dr. Albert Schäffle, who came from Württemberg, had been professor in Tübingen, and three years before had been called to Vienna as professor of national economy. To the end of his life this Suabian preacher of guild socialism, opponent of liberalism and capitalism, clung firmly to the conviction that the monarchy could only be saved by federalistic concessions.

The government created a model [for itself] in the concessions to the Poles along the lines of a federalistic decentralization. Once Kasimir von Grocholski had been named special minister without portfolio to represent the Galician interests in the central government (29 April 1871), the government began to broaden markedly the authority of the Galician *Landtag,* in which the Poles were dominant, at the expense of the central government. Extensive concessions were made to the autonomy of Galicia in the organization of the political administration on the local and intermediate levels, especially in the area of all higher and lower school administration. That as a result the Ruthenian element, powerless and underdeveloped as it was, together with the Germans was wholly delivered over to the authority of the Poles was felt to be less important than winning Polish cooperation and support in the central parliament. In 1871 the universities in Lemberg and Cracow were "Polonized," and the foundation of a Polish Academy of Science in Cracow was announced.

The government now thought to broaden fundamentally the autonomous authority of the Bohemian *Landtag* according to this Polish pattern, and thereby to fulfill one of the most important demands both of the federalism promoted by the nobility (Henry Count Clam-Martinic, Count Lebkowitz, Belcredi, etc.) and of national federalism. At the same time in this way something would also be done for states' rights. In the September Rescript (12 September 1871) Emperor Francis Joseph declared his readiness to recognize the legal position of the kingdom and to make this manifest through a coronation in Prague, and he encouraged the *Landtag* to work out proposals for a reconstruction of the relationship of Bohemia to the empire which would satisfy the legal claims of the land, on the one hand, and would damage neither the power position of the empire nor the claims of the other lands, on the other.

At the same time the government laid a nationality law before the *Landtag,* which contained the most generous concessions to the principle of equality. It prescribed the use of both languages in the laws of the land, in the proceedings of the *Landtag,* and in the composition of the proceedings; allowed the deputies to make use of either of the two languages according to the wish of each; and demanded that public officials should have a knowledge of both languages. For the purposes of administration and the election to representative bodies, the governmental districts should be divided as far as possible into uniform national areas; the local communities should have the right to determine the official language in governmental matters; in the districts, the official language of the district representation should be determined according to the language chosen by most of the local communities in the district. In order better to guarantee the equal rights of both nations, the *Landtag* should be divided into national curias with special responsibility for the national schools. These and a number of other provisions fully exhausted the possibilities of [national] equality.

Such an extensive satisfaction of the demands of the Czechs naturally contradicted the traditional privileged position of the Germans, or rather, of the dominant liberal class, and, what was more important, removed all limits on the pressure of the Czechs to broaden these concessions. On the other hand, no one saw at the time what considerable advantages were also offered to the Germans in the guarantee of their national position. That it meant a sacrifice for the German element there can be no doubt, [especially] if one considers what an overwhelmingly dominant position the Germans then possessed in Bohemia; but there should not have been any doubt that this sacrifice was a necessary and unavoidable consequence of historical and social development and the only means of creating a national-political situation which could bring new strength to the whole empire. The liberal-centralistic point of view of the "constitutionalists" who regarded every further development of the constitution as a threat to the fundamental principles of the empire (while in reality it was only a threat to the privileged position of the liberals) and of the now rapidly expanding group of German nationalists who caught fire from the impressive German victories against France was unable to adapt to the changed conditions of the empire.

The Germans walked out of the Bohemian *Landtag* and protested against the imperial rescript. The Czechs and federalists, however, worked out a response in agreement with the government, in which they drafted the foundations of a constitutional revision which have gone down in history as Fundamental Articles. Their basic purpose was to give to the lands of the crown of St. Wenceslas a similar position to that of Hungary, to broaden the compromise with Hungary to a Hungarian-Austrian-Bohemian Compromise, to change dualism into trialism. The central government should retain authority for common matters, foreign policy, army, and finance; the system of Delegations should be extended to Bohemia; all further matters, however, remained in principle the responsibility of the Bohemian government and legislature. Common matters, which could possibly include commerce and trade as well, should be the responsibility of a ministry consisting of departments [*Ressortministerien*], secretariat, or regional authorities.

One cannot of course judge how a system, outlined in the Fundamental Articles, of three nonsovereign, but independent, states and a superstate with such a complicated structure of authority would have functioned in practice. When one is aware of the difficulties which the dualistic system [had] already produced and correctly evaluates the tendency to further extension of independent authorities at the expense of the imperial unity, one is inclined to doubt [the possibility of] success. If, underlying the whole undertaking a dominant and directing state concept had been at work, one would have to concede to it Europeanwide significance.

In fact, however, the government retreated before the decided opposition of the German liberals and of the liberal Hungarian government, which did not want the [existing] constitution disturbed. If one only sees national-political motives underlying this opposition, then one does not do justice to the whole foreign and domestic problem of the monarchy at that time. Unquestionably concern about the consequences of such an experiment on the power position of the monarchy in Europe played an important role. One dare not underestimate the patriotic motive, even if egotistical power interests had much to say.

The emperor yielded to the pressure. The Hohenwart-Schäffle cabinet was dismissed. The ideas [which it sought to propagate] were too far-reaching for these men. Dualism remained the basis of the imperial constitution. It would have been correct to regard it [dualism] as the beginning of a constructive constitutional reform, but it became an unconquerable barrier and was in reality the premature end of a necessary process of development, a restrictive jacket, an unfinished thing. No one knew this better than the later heir to the throne, Francis Ferdinand, who was in his views at one with the loyal Hungarian politician Kristóffy, whose statesmanlike vision separated him, to his advantage, from so many Magyars: "Dualism is in its essence an introduction. It is the first step toward federalism. We must proceed in this fashion." These two dreamed of Austrian-Hungarian-Bohemian trialism and Hungarian-Croatian dualism as a constructive solution. Therein lay the secret of a new meaning for the monarchy, the realization of an idea that would have created a model of European significance.

This essay in practical politics represented the last attempt before the World War to find a constructive new order for the monarchy. For the Czechs the national-political ideas enunciated in the Declaration and in the Fundamental Articles formed the permanent guideline of their attitude and activities. When, in 1879, they gave up their fruitless policy of abstention and decided to enter the Reichsrat, they did so while reserving their constitutional position and with the determination to advance this position before a larger forum where a better prospect of producing results existed. The appearance of these fifty-six Czech deputies in the parliament changed its physiognomy and the power relationships of the parties immediately. More determined and united than the Germans, they placed their national objectives in the foreground and gave the deciding direction to the internal politics of the monarchy. That was the chief means of releasing increasingly national passions, of increasing the mutual suspicion between German and Czech to a poisonous level, which crippled and killed political reason.

The subsequent attempts of the [various] cabinets to bridge the ever more threatening conflict always fell apart on the basic difference of opinion over the constitutional question. . . . Graf Badeny (minister-president from 1895 to 1897) ordered the obligatory use of two languages by the officials of Bohemia and Moravia and therefore demanded from governmental officials proof of a knowledge of both tongues. By making the problem a purely administrative issue, he hoped to avoid the complications of a parliamentary discussion. This attempt was in fact foreshadowed by similar efforts of Taaffe and Stremayr (1880). But since the Germans, with a previously unheard-of unanimity, rejected this solution of the problem, which had been arrived at by one-sided agreement with the Czechs, while the Czechs declared that it was merely one stage in the realization of their final constitutional aims, the constitutional and national [in the larger sense] character of the issue was brought clearly to light. The conflict totally paralyzed the work of the legislative bodies. There was no

FIGURE 5. ''Hey, Vincey, how are they giving you your orders now, in German or in Bohemian?'' ''Oh, our orders are in German, so we'll learn it, but we're chewed out in Bohemian, so we'll understand it!'' *(Cartoon by J. B. Engl,* Simplicissimus *12 JHRG. No. 8 (1907))*

escape other than to withdraw the regulations, to restore the status quo. Ernst von Koerber (1900–1904) sought in vain to find a new way out.

That, however, certain possibilities existed is shown in the relative success of the compromise negotiations in Moravia (1905) and in the Bukovina (1910). Here a national registry was created, which underlay the exercise of the right of election to the *Landtag.* The *Landtage* were divided into national curias; the provinces [*Länder*] were divided into independent national electoral districts, so that a community belonged at the same time to the one and to the other group, while the voter was only allowed to vote with his nationality [personality principle]. In the case of a number of decisions of national significance a two-thirds majority was required, so that the minority could not be "majoritized." The use of the local tongue on the part of the autonomous administrations and school supervision by national cultural officials was provided for. That this path could be followed with success even in the four-tongued land, Bukovina, with its four religious affiliations, demonstrated the possibilities of an idea that attempted to solve the problem regionally, without bringing the national constitution into it. That was, however, the core of the problem; for regional agreements could calm and soothe the provinces, but not the peoples. The nationality problem revealed itself ever more decisively as a problem of the imperial constitution, in which the problem of the constitutional security of the national minorities was embedded as essential substance.

The opinion had prevailed that the introduction of universal, direct, equal suffrage would also calm the national waters. In fact this new regulation of the year 1907 fulfilled one of the most important demands of the Slavs, namely that of political equality, just like the democratic demand of social equality. What could a Slav in Austria still demand? There were no formal special rights for any nation. Every Austrian, to whatever nationality he belonged, was equal before the same law, had full freedom of movement, enjoyed the same freedom in intellectual and material respects. Each had a share in the Great Power position of the monarchy, in the natural riches of her products, in the many varied wonders of her natural beauty. From the variety of her many peoples and of their spiritual qualities, of the national temperament, the capabilities and talents of her citizens developed unimaginable riches in the form of inspiration, relations, experiences, possibilities for mutual cooperation and fulfillment, for finding pleasure in life with which the poverty of our present existence offers no comparison. There were still unsatisfied wishes, enough unsolved complications, there were very real concerns, passions and suffering, there was a sufficiency of social differences, but all that affected not just one nation within Austria and it was not the problem of Austria alone.

What was the reason that even the democratization of voting produced no alteration, but rather the struggle of the nationalities continued with no change of intensity? Because outside the monarchy a development had occurred which stood in sharp contrast to the universal supranational concept of the Austrian state; because the Austrian state problem was tied in with the rivalries of the European powers, with the drive towards imperialism, and with the conflicts of world politics. Serbian, Rumanian, Italian nationalism, which strove for the most complete inclusion of territories inhabited by fellow nationals, exercised a steadily rising influence on the nationalities of Austria. The Entente powers could see in the internal difficulties of the ally of the German Empire a factor which played into their hands. Not for nothing did foreigners who previously knew little enough of the internal conditions of the monarchy busy themselves with the nationality problem, relying mostly on one-sided materials with a specific objective in mind, stemming from the radical national German or Slavic camp. Thus such slogans as "prison of peoples" or "subjugation of the nations," which awakened untrue or exaggerated suspicions, have remained firmly fixed in Western historical literature.

Joseph Redlich

THE COMPROMISE OF 1867: CONSTITUTIONAL STRAITJACKET

A liberal analyst of Austria's constitutional problem, Redlich holds the Compromise of 1867 to be no "compromise" but rather a major constitutional disaster, confining the imperial government in a legal straitjacket from which it could never win release.

If we look once more at the history of the Austrian imperial problem since the outbreak of the March Revolution [in 1848] . . . the decisive characteristics of the whole picture become clear from all the contending historical forces, ideas, and tendencies. The most striking feature of the whole struggle conducted by the Magyar-dominated

From Joesph Redlich, *Das österreichische Staats- und Reichsproblem* (Vienna, 1926), vol. 2, pp. 672–680.

Hungary [to assure] its position in the empire is the fact that from the very beginning this struggle was carried out with and against the dynasty, while the people of the western half of the empire remained politically inactive in the face of the rapidly intensifying struggle, in fact through their continued willingness to serve in the imperial army offered the dynasty the means of overcoming and suppressing the Hungarians. Only the short-lived democracy of Vienna in 1848 felt solidarity towards the struggle for freedom of the followers of Kossuth, because it hoped thereby to forestall the dictatorship which threatened it. [But] the majority of the Constituent Assembly of 1848 under German leadership expressly supported the policy of restoring the full power of imperial authority against the separatist tendencies of the Hungarian constitution of April 1848, a policy represented by the government of Dr. Alexander Bach.

The markedly absolutist features of the attitude of the young as well as the mature emperor, Francis Joseph, are in the last analysis the main reason that the imperial problem remained an issue which at the end existed between him and the Magyars. For after the establishment of unlimited personal rule in 1851, only his will counted in all Hungarian questions; only from time to time, and without publicity, did he allow the top Hungarian aristocracy, the group of old conservatives, to explain to him their political plans and goals. The same individuals were the ones whom he, at the beginning very reluctantly, recognized as an interest group qualified to negotiate in the period following the defeat of 1859. But when the offer of mediation revealed itself to have no purpose, the governing circles in the palace in Vienna decided forthwith to dissolve the Reichstag in Pest before that body had had time to present its constitutional arguments in the first Address [to the monarch].

But when concern over foreign-policy developments—and it was these almost exclusively—compelled the monarch to [initiate] new negotiations with the Magyars, it was again the leaders of the upper aristocracy to whom he at first listened. The suspension of the February constitution in 1865 had the primary purpose of protecting the emperor against any intervention of the Austrian peoples, especially the German constitutional party, in the negotiations over the Compromise. The new order for the empire should be established between king and Hungarian Reichstag alone; that was Francis Joseph's point of view just as it was the idea of the Magyars, arising from their drive for independence.

It is difficult to believe that Francis Deák himself ever thought seriously of submitting the Compromise, already concluded with the emperor and his government of bureaucrats, to a vote of the Viennese Reichsrat over its actual contents, or even to regard the opinion of the Reichsrat as other than a mere formality. Consequently, despite the loss of prestige which Austria suffered in the war with Prussia, despite the embitterment of the constitutional party and its followers over the Belcredi regime, despite the excitement [prevailing] among the Czechs, the affair developed as planned: the emperor Francis Joseph, supported exclusively by his government of bureaucrats, concluded the final peace treaty with the majority of the Hungarian Reichstag, whose existence half a generation earlier he had declared to be forfeit.

The recognition of these Hungarian rights in the form in which the April constitution of 1848 had expressed them, likewise the recognition by an independent Hungary of the immediate diplomatic and military sovereignty of the common ruler over the entire empire is, seen from the Austrian point of view, as exclusively the work of the emperor as the original content of that [April] constitution had been, in the first place, the work of Louis Kossuth.

To be sure: it was the Kossuth of the March Days, the ministerial colleague of Francis Deák, who had created this constitution, not the Kossuth who as governor in 1849 had announced the final dethroning of Francis Joseph and the dynasty. Since, however, Kossuth, although in exile, always remained "the governor," he at first felt himself to be beaten. Over his head the scion of the royal house against which he had tirelessly conspired carried off the victory. Still, Francis Joseph had created the Compromise with the help of the former liberal comrades of Louis Kossuth, who thereby reestablished the April constitution—henceforth with a text changed in only a few places —and with it an independent Hungary. At the same time, [these same comrades of Kossuth] had so changed this constitution, through the express recognition of the [existence of] common affairs [affecting both parts of the empire] and through the creation of institutions necessary to take care of these common matters [the delegations], that it became an effective instrument for the emperor and king, now committed to dualism.

It is one of the most fateful consequences of Vienna's newly restored absolutism of 1851, an absolutism created without effective opposition, that from that point on a peaceful solution of the imperial problem by means of the cooperative effort of all the peoples of the monarchy became impossible. Francis Joseph's firmly held policy of treating Hungary as a province, compelled to fit into the imperial structure through military power, had the effect that, far beyond official circles, the strongest political and social element in the Austria of that time, the German middle class, as well as the German-minded aristocracy, fell more and more under the influence of the official doctrine, especially since the economic interests of the middle class unquestionably harmonized with [this doctrine]. As a result the opinion spread to practically all elements of the Austrian population except the masses, whatever their nationality, that the maintenance of the empire as a closed political and administrative entity was just as much their interest as that of the dynasty.

Viewed in this way the acceptance of the February constitution was merely the expression of the fact that the education of the Austrian Germans by the absolutist regime in centralistic imperial thought had achieved everything that could be wished. The weakness of the liberal constitutional legislation of Schmerling corresponded only too well to the powerlessness of the political life which it unleashed. Not the suffrage according to census groupings, which excluded the urban masses, but rather the rudimentary political nature of the Germans of Austria, who were almost the only actors on the newly erected parliamentary stage, was responsible for the general apathy of the broadest circles towards politics and, especially, for the attitude towards the imperial constitutional problem. The small but powerful group of knowledgeable people with the strongest interest in the maintenance of imperial unity, the representatives of Viennese and Bohemian industry, consoled themselves with the conviction that the bureaucracy of Vienna was after all best able to care for their interests.

Under these circumstances it was a simple thing for the emperor, and one which accorded well with his nature, to keep the reconstruction of the Hungarian relationship wholly in his own hands. One does not need to emphasize that the most important opinions and principles of his bureaucratic ministers, especially in questions of finance and economics, did not stand in the way of the absolutist tendencies of the monarch, particularly in the sphere of higher policy of which the imperial problem formed a part. [These bureaucrats], in fact, could scarcely influence the course of events.

In actuality the Hungarians' struggle for their rights was from the beginning a double battle: if Deák was, from 1861 on, the undisputed leader and the creative political will of Hungary, the emperor and his ministers played the same role on the other side. Thus the decision of the emperor at the critical point in the struggle—as was so often the case during his reign—was made with the suddenness of a purely personal conclusion. In the first days of January 1867 the prospects for an understanding between the Vienna government and the leaders of the compromise party in Budapest were slight. The ministerial draft [of an agreement] over common matters was described by Andrássy as unacceptable, and at just that moment the emperor revealed through the over-hasty issuance of a new defense law how far he still thought in absolutist terms. But as early as January 15 the negotiations of the Austrian minister and the delegates of the Deák party began to look promising. The fact that, at this point, the draft of the Committee of Fifteen of the Hungarian Reichstag, in place of the Austrian draft, became the basis of negotiations indicates that the decision of the emperor had already been made. From that point on all the inner circles knew of the change in Hungary's favor. For Francis Joseph was in the meantime personally persuaded that the same amount of military power would be his as common commander-in-chief as he had hitherto had in a unitary empire. This was the decisive question for him: everything else appeared to him as secondary and insignificant.

If one asked who emerged victorious in this struggle, then public opinion in Austria unanimously, and from the beginning, designated the Hungarians as such. And this view soon became the public opinion of all Europe. The more the rising influence of Hungary became apparent under the dualistic regime, the more its preponderance in the policy-making decisions of the Habsburg monarchy became evident, the more this judgment became firmly rooted and remained so to the last days of the empire.

Now there can be no doubt that the Compromise of 1867 was only brought into being because the emperor suddenly departed from the policy to which he had held firm for two decades. The wisdom and forethought of Deák's tactics also make clear that the former attitude of the majority of the Hungarian Reichstag with its emphasis on the Magyar idea of national independence faded into the background as, through this change of heart on the part of the emperor, the Hungarians were won over to accepting the Great Power position of the monarchy and of the dynasty [as a necessary element of any settlement]. Only the future could show whether the old empire of the Habsburgs, now reconstructed on the basis of a "dualism of equality," in fact possessed in the common institutions the possibility of maintaining itself as a European Great Power; further whether the economic and political development of both halves of the empire could be assured in the newly created structure. That both Francis Deák and Francis Joseph felt this assurance in the days of their agreement cannot be doubted. Nevertheless one may certainly doubt—without doing the emperor an injustice—whether Francis Joseph, in line with his whole character as ruler, was personally wholly convinced when he concluded the Compromise that he had created a fact which henceforth could neither be changed nor overturned. The way in which he had, hitherto, adopted "governmental systems" and then abandoned them, issued constitutions and then suspended them, gives ground for doubt whether he may not have concluded his pact with the Hungarians in January 1867 with inner reservations to return under more favorable circumstances in the future to the centralistic idea and thus reestablish the full measure of his imperial prerogative, even in Hungary. Because in the last analysis the self-limitations which he now laid on himself for the benefit of the Magyars rested wholly on his judgment of the changed European power relationships produced by the war with Prussia and Italy, whose results were so very much to the disadvantage of the House of Habsburg. It was precisely this which compelled him at that moment to pacify the Hungarians politically and to gather together and strengthen the military and economic potential of the whole empire as the basis for a future, more successful, foreign policy. Seen from this point of view, dualism as a constitution first achieved "full legal validity" two years later, when, in the months of August and September 1870, the collapse of the Second Empire in France extinguished forever in Emperor Francis Joseph all hopes of a possible revenge for the defeat dealt out to him by the victorious Hohenzollern dynasty.

Thus the policy of Emperor Francis Joseph followed other paths than those which the prior period of his regime would have led one to expect. From that point on no one protected the dualistic solution of the imperial problem so carefully as the emperor and king. The feeling of obligation toward the coronation oath which he had carried out, of which there was much talk during the later political struggles between crown and Magyars, probably coincided in Francis Joseph's mind with the view that the dualistic organization of his empire, which he had created, despite its obvious weaknesses and shortcomings in many directions, was still the sole method of keeping together his inheritance.

The personal commitment of the emperor to the Compromise of 1867 had, however, one particularly far-reaching consequence, since he found himself compelled to hold firm, not merely to the form of the dualistic imperial constitution, but to its underlying concept as the political determinant in both halves of the empire. This underlying concept said that just as in Hungary, the Magyars, so in the western half of the empire, the Germans counted as the bearers of the imperial idea expressed in dualism and, accordingly, were called upon to play the corresponding leadership role among the peoples of the empire. In Hungary this idea was not merely carried through right from the beginning, but was maintained with steadily rising force and unscrupulousness against the non-Magyar nationalities of the Hungarian state. In Austria, on the other hand, this guiding principle of imperial politics began to waver within two years of the re-creation of the German constitutional party as the ruling parliamentary party; and as early as 1871, with the appointment of the Hohenwart ministry, Francis Joseph began to consider the thought of a federal reconstruction of the consitution in the western half of the empire, and appeared thereby, to the Hungarian statesmen, to be threatening in substantial measure the basic—and for them indispensible—conditions of the dualistic structure. Under Andrássy's leadership the opposition of the Deák party in Hungary to the new course in Austria, in combination with the opposition of the liberal German middle classes (powerfully encouraged by the imperial chancellor Count Beust) and the centralistically minded group of the nobility, succeeded in bringing the whole experiment to a halt. Thus for a further seven years the system of a joint German and Magyar hegemony as a basis for the dualistic imperial policy remained in force. But when Francis Joseph, with the appointment of Count Taaffe, introduced a complete and lasting change in the internal politics of Austria and brought about the unavoidable fall of the political supremacy of the Germans in the western half of the empire, he in fact brought the basic idea of the dualistic imperial policy into ever sharper conflict with the actual power relationships of the nationalities and with the whole political and social structure of the Austrian half of the empire.

The course of "undermining" the dualistic principle, as Deák formulated it, appears to one looking back on the fifty years of further life of the empire as inevitable. This "undermining" became unavoidable because the Compromise had from the beginning merely signified the artificial freezing of the power relationships and the political, national, and economic conflicts in precisely that form in which they momentarily found themselves at the end of the war of 1866. The institutions created at the beginning of 1867 as a permanent imperial structure operated, therefore, on the further development of the special interests of nationalities and classes in both halves of the empire, as well as on the rising national consciousness of the non-German and non-Magyar peoples, as an increasingly unbearable pressure, like an iron frame, which checked in purely mechanical fashion the struggle of the peoples and classes not destined for power to achieve political recognition. The introduction of universal manhood suffrage in Austria in 1907 and its consequence, the permanent weakening of the hegemony of the Germans by the remaining nationalities in the central parliament on the one hand, the irrepressible rise of Kossuthean notions of independence among the Magyars on the other, indicate clearly the extremes of development to which political circumstances had driven the empire from that starting point of the firmly established concept of dualism created by Deák and the emperor in 1867.

Thus reference is made to that cause, which determined the fragility of the Compromise from the outset: the contrasting approach of both halves of the new dualistic monarchy to the nationality problem. While in Hungary the re-creation of the constitution led directly to the creation of a centralized, exclusively Magyar governmental system, which left in force the historical self-government of the *Comitates* [county councils] only insofar as these forms of autonomy proved themselves suitable tools for the complete exclusion of the remaining nationalities from government and administration, in Austria the constitutional work of 1867 merely confirmed once more the principle of equality of the nationalities with respect to their languages. And although the German constitutional party remained in power for a decade, it nevertheless did not anchor the actual predominance of the German language in the constitution. The party contented itself with keeping intact that official language which derived from the era of absolutism, by which the superiority of German as in fact the national language appeared to be sufficiently insured. [Yet] the gradual broadening of the parliamentary suffrage in a democratic sense in Austria, in combination with the extension of the autonomous institutions created by the constitution for the provinces and communities, led to a complete democratization and nationalization of political life as well as of public administration in the entire western half of the empire, by which the strengthening of the non-German nationalities and the weakening of the centralistic political attitudes and of the political power of the Germans became unmistakable. While Austria, at the beginning of the second decade of the twentieth century, appeared to the observer looking beneath the surface as a complex of developing national units, with effort held together in the form of the historic unitary state, at the same time the complete elimination in Hungary of the language as well as the political rights of the non-Magyar peoples, who were in the majority, led to the establishment in the whole Hungarian Kingdom of a national unitary state whose entire political structure, as well as the spirit of its legislation and administration, contradicted the basic elements dominating the scene in Austria in the public life of all its peoples in all respects. That in one and the same empire such contradictory developments could come to fruition—despite unceasing conflicts between both governments and unrelenting controversy among the political and national parties in both halves—without leading to a dissolution of the union or to a collapse of the empire is to be ascribed, both as responsibility and as service, to the emperor and king, Francis Joseph.

The emperor thus raised the unchanged maintenance of the Compromise of 1867 to the actual foundation of his policy, and let this be ever more unmistakably known, and thus that which had been a momentary assist to dynastic power politics became stabilized as the purest "reason of state." In this way he placed the Compromise in the center of the conflicts for political and social recognition on the part of all the advancing nationalities of his empire. Consequently it was merely the result of unyielding historical and political logic that in the moment when the moth-eaten empire of the Habsburgs tottered towards collapse, undermined by four years of war and even more by the propaganda directed at its nationalities by the enemy states, the call for the dissolution of the empire was given by the last leading statesman of the Magyars, Count Stephen Tisza. With the destruction of the power of the Habsburg-Lothringian dynasty both the imperial concept which it incorporated and the justification for the existence of the

Magyar national "empire" established on the basis of dualism were extinguished. Thus the accomplishment of 1867, after a half century of operating as the basis for dynastic Great Power politics, drove its two creators, the dynasty and the imperial Hungarians, simultaneously with the ruin of German power in Europe, into the abyss.

III NEW FORCES, INDUSTRIALISM, SOCIALISM, AND WORLD WAR I

With the Compromise of 1867 the era of constitutional experimentation came to an end. From that point onward the impetus to imperial unity came overwhelmingly from nongovernmental sources. Taking advantage of the breakdown of provincial barriers in the economic reforms of Bruck, industrialists and entrepreneurs began to exploit the rich potential of the Austro-Hungarian market. The vast agricultural resources of the Hungarian plain were complemented by the long tradition of craftsmanship in the small towns of Bohemia as well as by the new factories springing up around the capital. These latter brought with them an emerging industrial proletariat whose interests, vis-à-vis the employers, cut across national ties. Thus the empire became once more a society of classes whose antagonisms, though no less bitter, began to override the ethnic differences.

Heinrich Benedikt
THE SPREAD OF INDUSTRIALISM

In this selection Heinrich Benedikt (b. 1886), a professor at the University in Vienna and a prolific author, analyzes Austria's modern industrial development, revealing the extent to which economic interests were beginning to break down local ties, though the restrictive power of these ties remained great. Benedikt's views on economics are astonishingly appropriate for the era of which he writes, for he is an unabashed admirer of the virtues of private enterprise.

The alternation of seven fat and seven lean years, proclaimed by the Egyptian Joseph, referred to long experience of the Pharaonic market. [Nonetheless], what was recognized on the Nile also took place on the Seine, the Thames, the Hudson, the Spree, and the Danube. In Austria in the summer of 1866 a seven-year sequence of fat years set in, coming to a sudden end on Friday, 9 May 1873.

The hearts of the men who had experienced Königgrätz, as well as those of their sons, bled at the memory of the lost war. They could not get over the blows of 1859, 1866, and 1867: the defeats of Magenta and Solferino, the loss of Lombardy, the catastrophe on the Bohemian battlefield, the sacrifice of Venetia, the exclusion from Germany, and the division of the empire into two parts by means of the unsatisfying Compromise. [But] viewed coolly these blows of fate constitute an operation which freed the suffering body from three problems it was too weak to master. Unburdened of concern for the defense of the Italian provinces, freed through total separation from the rivalry with Prussia, reconciled with the Magyars after a twenty-year trial of strength, the Danube Monarchy could [now] dedicate itself to building up its economy, to unfolding its rich resources.

The seven fat years began with a record harvest, such as had not been known in the memory of men. The railroads could scarcely manage to transport the tremendous quantities of grain to western Europe, which was afflicted by a harvest failure, where they were sold for high prices. The railroads were forced to increase their rolling stock. New lines arose, and the iron and steel industry, after several

From Heinrich Benedikt, *Die wirtschaftliche Entwicklung in der Franz-Joseph-Zeit* (Vienna and Munich, 1958), pp. 79–81, 83, 85, 88–89, 91, 92, 159–60, 172–173, 173–175, 176. Translated by permission of Herold Druck–und Verlagsgesellschaft m.b.H.

years of undercapacity operation, was delighted with the many new orders. 1867 was the best year of the Danube Shipping Company from its founding until the present time.

> *The progress of foreign exchange [in Austria] is dependent on the export of grain; the income sources of all [Austrian] railroads are conditioned by that export. However, rich harvests have a favorable effect on the stock market, so that savings are in large measure invested in new shares.*

The predominance of Hungary as the bread basket of Europe over the rapidly industrializing Austria was revealed in the customs treaty with Prussia on 9 March 1868 and the supplementary agreement negotiated by Beust on 1 July with England. Concerned by the rising imports from England, the Austrian industrialists pressed for new negotiations which led to an agreement accepted by both parliaments, but with exceptional readiness by the Hungarian, since it assured custom-free entry for grain [into England]. This supplementary agreement [ratified on] 30 December 1869 was the last success of the free trade movement. The supplementary convention with England eliminated duties on men's clothing fabrics and drove the industry of Brünn [Brno] into a tight spot; Brünn took over the leadership of the reaction against free trade. . . .

The great event for the shipping of Triest was the opening of the Suez Canal. Triest was the nearest large harbor of significance to Alexandria. The major part of the Egyptian cotton production was exported by way of Triest, a considerable quantity was spun in the Alpine districts and in Bohemia. . . . At the opening of the Suez Canal (1869) Francis Joseph, garbed in a green walking coat, white stockings, and a straw hat, led the empress Eugénie [of France] on his arm, followed by the khedive [of Egypt] and the crown prince of Prussia. England sent only the ambassador to Turkey. The festival opera commissioned by the khedive, the immortal *Aida,* had as its theme a sad story not exactly appropriate to the festival occasion. A thousand Austrians had worked on the canal['s construction], among them many Dalmatians, fellow clansmen of the insurgents whose cruelties against imperial soldiers in the Crivoscie were still fresh in many memories. Nonetheless, they were allowed to form the emperor's bodyguard. On the day of the dedication of the canal in Port Said the marriage of the aged de Lesseps with the duchess of Alba, a niece of the empress Eugénie, took place.

The screw steamer *Narenta* was the first ship through the canal into the Red Sea. Immediately after the opening of the canal the [Austrian] Lloyd instituted a regular service to Bombay with two steamers, each of 1200 tons. . . . In 1869 the [Lloyd] company possessed over sixty-three steamships with 59,000 registered tons. In 1880 the Bombay line was extended to Singapore and Hong Kong, and in order to bring the jute export to Triest, voyages to Calcutta were instituted.

In 1879 Lloyd paid the largest dividend of its life. . . .

The export of grain, flour, and sugar benefited the currency and the improved currency benefited the credit of the government. The economic flowering, the influx of gold, the reduction of the interest level on the world markets made possible the unification of a variety of governmental obligations—industrial subvention loans, domestic debentures, national and lottery loans, government bonds, and others —into a single government bond issue; in the conversion savings of 83 million gulden were achieved. The credit of the monarchy had so improved that, in the course of the year 1867, the 1864 lottery shares rose from 74 to 113 gulden. The law of 20 June 1868 laid a coupon tax of 16 percent on the 5 percent unified debt, which had the effect of lowering the interest rate to 4.2 percent. This was regarded as a proceeding damaging the interests of the creditors, and it was only the intervention of James Rothschild, at the instance of the ambassador Beust, which prevented the Austrian debt certificates from being banned by the Paris stock market.

Thanks to the growing prosperity and the increase of tax [revenue] the budget improved. The upswing of the grain trade, whose central point still lay in Vienna, as well as a series of legal disputes led to the creation of an arbitration court for the fruit and flour exchange, the first specialized commercial court in Austria. In the realm of legislation the bankruptcy regulation of 25 December 1868, deserves mention. . . .

On the first of May [1873] the yet unfinished world exposition was opened by the imperial couple in the company of the German crown prince and the Prince of Wales. From the very beginning the exposition disappointed the hopes which had been placed on it, less through the outbreak of cholera, which reduced the number of wealthy visitors for whose reception the new hotels, especially the luxurious Grand Hotel, had been outfitted, than through the frightful stock market crisis of 9 May 1873, Black Friday. The panic in and in front of the provisional building on the *Schottenring,* opposite the stock market building of Hansen which was still under construction, was indescribable, despite the fact that the number of annual admission cards for the stock market visitors had risen from 867 in 1867 to 2352. The word "crash" was first applied to the stock market crisis of 1873, appearing in the stock market report of a Viennese newspaper, whose reporter supposedly took it from the remarks of a visitor from Galicia. . . .

The consequences of Black Friday were somewhat modified by the temporary suspension of the Bank Act, by the creation of prepayment accounts [for commerce], by modification of the rules on bank mergers, and by extension of the tax exemption for new construction, the Danube regulation and the Vienna high spring aqueduct, but the economic depression lingered on and first reached its peak in the period between autumn 1875 and autumn 1876. The reduced harvests, the weakened purchasing power of the agricultural population, the general mistrust, the numerous bankruptcies, the devaluation of silver and the rise of the gold premium, which caused trade to lose the basis of firm calculations, the breakdown of the Compromise negotiations with Hungary, the revolt in Bosnia and the Eastern Question, the rising deficit and the sinking value of government obligations characterize this period. In 1873 stock averages fell from 339 to 196 and at the end of 1876 reached their lowest point of 105. Only in the year 1877, with the renewal of the Compromise, the rich harvest, the disappearance of the danger of a European war into which the monarchy would be drawn, did the four years of stagnation come to an end. . . .

Black Friday unleashed—like the *Kredit-Anstalt* crisis of 1931—a world crisis that reached its peak in New York where it was created by the overrapid development of the railways and heavy industry. The catastrophic character of the Vienna crisis lay in the fact that the speculation was confined to the country rather than being spread out on the world markets and that in Austria the gambling passion, by means of the little lotto, the lottery shares, and the fluctuations of foreign exchange, became vastly enlarged and weakened the saving tendencies. . . .

The strongest bond which held the two states [Austria and Hungary] together in their economic community was the cartels. In the area of heavy industry the common customs area was maintained through common cartels after long, bitter competitive struggles. The cartels performed the same service for other industries.

In 1886 the first Austrian-Hungarian iron cartel was created, in 1888 the soda cartel, in 1890 the copper wire, in 1892 the enamel ware and petroleum cartels were established, 1894 saw the copper rolling works cartel, 1896 a new iron cartel, 1897 produced the starch cartel, the year 1899 the jute, the coach, the rubber and oil cloth cartels, and in 1911 the common sugar cartel emerged.

The cartels insured the common customs area. International cartels, for which Austria and Hungary offer the outstanding examples, and for which national cartels are a precondition, contradict through their many blessings the supposed advantages of the anticartel legislation of the United States. Reference to Hungarian competition was the decisive influence which from the beginning prevented Austria's introduction of a cartel law.

The great machine-tool works, the chemical and food industries [of Hungary] were controlled by the General Hungarian Credit Bank, which belonged to the Rothschild and *Kredit-Anstalt* interests. The Hungarian Commercial Bank of Pest, with its large industrial holdings, was founded with Austrian and, to a small degree, German capital. The prime factor which moved the Hungarians when the mere threat of a division of the empire for customs purposes was raised was the common character of the money market, which served Hungarian purposes exclusively. Without the aid of the Viennese Rothschild group the Hungarians could scarcely have marketed the government loans.

The colonization and the industrialization of Hungary are the work of the ruling house of Austria and of Viennese financial and industrial capital. . . . [Nevertheless], substantial disadvantages counterbalanced the inestimable advantages of the unified economic system of the monarchy. There was only one customs area, but within this two governments, and of these Hungary's was without question much stronger politically. The layout of the Hungarian railroad lines, with the center in Budapest, the Hungarian tariff policy with its equivalent of export premiums, governmental subventions for Hungarian factories, the customs duties designed specifically with Hungarian interests in mind, and the substantially smaller burden of social charges [in Hungary as compared with Austria] had the result that Austrian industry suffered more from Hungarian than foreign competition. The Hungarian government was supported by its legislature, the Austrian, thanks to the political incapacity of the legislature there, was either restricted [in its accomplishments] or driven, through regard for the wishes of a temporary majority, in a direction inimical to industry.

While in the Hungarian half of the empire the dominance of the Hungarian nation became evident in the economic field, immediately after the settlement of the Hungarian question in the Compromise of 1867 Austria was subjected to the diverging pressures of the Czech struggle against German enterprise. . . . The Czech deputies employed all their influence within the government to insure that government commissions and contracts came to Czech firms. Czech deliveries to state enterprises advanced hand in hand with the systematic "Czechisization" of the railroad administration, the post office, and other government installations. . . . It was a sign of national virtue to buy more expensive things abroad rather than the same things more cheaply from a German. The historian who seeks the truth often finds it in the courtroom. Courtroom proceedings are the most reliable sources, and the Kestranek case offers an outstanding example of this extreme national chauvinism.

In 1908 the city of Prague and the neighboring communities decided to build a water conduit. The Iron-Industry Firm of Prague offered pipes, transport charges inclusive, at 18.85 kroner per 100 kg; the French firm Schneider-Creuzot in Pont-à-Mousson [France] at 21.95 kroner. The administrative council of the water works, formed of representatives of the city of Prague and the neighboring communities, assigned the contract to Pont-à-Mousson. The national veneer which was supposed to justify the boycott of a firm with a German-Austrian president and headquarters in Vienna lacked solid foundations, since the French firm belonged in large measure to German interests (Haldy & Co. and Röchling Brothers in Saarbrücken), and the principal sufferer was the pipe casting works of Prague Iron in Königshof [a suburb of Prague], where only Czech workers were employed. The loss in wages for the Czech workers amounted to 700,000 kroner. The award of the contract to the French firm had as its consequence demonstrations of Prague's unemployed who demanded bread and work.

The corruption of Czech authorities was hidden under the cloak of national interest. The Prague Iron Works had been promised the contract if it was prepared to offer the city officials entrusted with the water works administration a commission of 5 percent and the middleman an additional 2 percent. The central director Wilhelm Kestranek revealed the facts to the *Prager Tageblatt,* which published his letter in a lead article on 27 August 1908, whereupon the city council, the city assembly, and Dr. Černohorský felt obliged to sue Kestranek for libel. Dr. Černohorský was Reichsrat deputy, city assemblyman, and president of the water works commission and was the one who had appeared, without identifying himself, in the Vienna office of Prague Iron Works to negotiate the commission. His identity could easily be established from a photograph in the Reichsrat almanac, and since he knew that his name was known he appeared personally to institute the libel proceedings. The case began before the jury court in Prague on 5 February 1909 and concluded after four days with the condemnation of Kestranek to pay a fine of 3000 kroner for libel of the city council and the city assembly. He was pronounced innocent of libeling Dr. Černohorský.

The case throws garish light on the nationality question. . . . The jury declared that it had no command of German and requested to be relieved of its duty should the accused be allowed to answer in German. According to the language regulations introduced by Stremayer, the accused had the right [to demand] the conduct of the proceedings in German, but he renounced this right to avoid delay. His defense attorney merely demanded that the most important statements [of the accusers] should be immediately translated into German.

Had Kestranek's letter been published in Reichenberg or Eger or Vienna instead of Prague and the charge therefore brought in other than a Czech court, Kestranek would have been unanimously declared not guilty, but for the average Czech citizen [Kleinbürger] the acceptance of a "commission" by a fellow countryman in public office was quite all right, especially when it was a question of money from the hated Germans. To be sure, the Czech jury did not go so far as to support the Czech Reichsrat deputy, Černohorský, who had so unwisely allowed himself to be identified. . . .

[Nonetheless,] the nationality conflicts which so adversely affected economic life would in all probability, even without the war, have been modified, had the monarchy continued to exist, into a healthy, productive competition, since the social inequalities which were the actual cause of the evil were rapidly disappearing.

National hatred is really a law unto itself. You'll always find it most strongly felt on the lowest level of culture. But there's a point at which it [such hatred] wholly disappears, and one responds to the fortune or misfortune of the neighboring people as if it were that of one's own. (Goethe)

Hans Rosenberg

THE CANCER OF INDUSTRIAL DEPRESSION

In his brilliant analysis of the effects of economics on politics, Hans Rosenberg (b. 1904), who was trained in Germany but has long been a resident in the United States and has been professor of history at the University of California at Berkeley since 1959, shows how world-wide economic changes had their effects on the Austrian economy and, by slowing economic expansion, exacerbated Austria's ethnic conflicts. Rosenberg's economic pessimism contrasts with the economic optimism underlying Benedikt's work.

Just as the depression years of 1873 to 1878 introduced a long-range change in the cyclical as well as, in part, in the structural tendencies of economic development in central Europe, their immediate political consequence . . . meant, in its effects, much more than a purely temporary reaction to the liberal dominance and the rise of industrial social classes. This was the beginning of the end of the "age of liberalism," and of the hegemony of the individualistic economic and social philosophy. For there can be no doubt that the crisis and the decline of economic liberalism in imperial Germany and in German Austria, as well as the weakening and disintegration of political liberalism is one of the outstanding and most historically significant developments in central Europe during the Great Depression. . . .

Broad historical perspectives reveal themselves, not merely in imperial Germany, but also in the Danube Monarchy if one seeks out the reasons for the character of the period between 1873 and 1896, especially when one examines in particular the effects of the prolonged decline of business prosperity as well as the short-term shifts in the economy on the regrouping of the social, political, and ideological forces and the [consequent] reconstruction of public life. . . . If one compares the paths pursued in Austria with the solutions attempted in imperial Germany, significant differences emerge along with many similarities, although the decisive historical results remain in essence the same: in both central European empires advancing industrialism did not lead to a lasting and healthy consolidation of the existing

From Hans Rosenberg, *Grosse Depression und Bismarckzeit* (Berlin, 1967), pp. 62, 227–252. Translated by permission of Walter de Gruyter & Co.

social structure and of the political dominance [of its leading elements]. These parallel historical developments can be judged according to the Biblical principle: "By their fruits shall ye know them."

If one starts with the simple facts of Austrian social policy and the conflict with the "presumptuous" industrial proletariat in particular, as this developed on the governmental level and under the stress of the cyclical decline and the [resulting] socioeconomic competition, one encounters a contrast which, in comparison with imperial Germany, is more sharply drawn, both negatively and positively. The more extreme fluctuation between governmental suppression and constructive social measures was typical of Austria, a thoroughly contradictory mixture of brutal repression and promising efforts at understanding. This state of affairs requires an explanation, especially since political initiative in the area of social policy lay, in the years after 1878, with the aristocratic possessors of vast estates, social conservatives; even at the turn of the century the preindustrial forces predominated in the economy, and the shift of economic power to industry and finance capital remained far behind that of imperial Germany.

Although the volume of industrial output per capita rose markedly in Germany in the course of the Great Depression, and by the mid-1890s industry had superseded agriculture in terms of the percentage of the population employed in it, the Austrian half of the Habsburg Empire exhibited a decided tendency towards stagnation in this period, especially as revealed in the percentages of the population earning their living in agriculture, industry, and handicrafts. In 1867, 67 percent of Austrian employees were occupied in agriculture; in 1890, 62 percent; and in 1900 agriculture still employed 58 percent. In 1867, 20 percent; in 1890, 20 percent; and in 1900, 21 percent found employment in industry. Only in commerce and transportation, especially in the overdeveloped area of small stores, is a sharp rise to be seen: here the percentages were 4 percent in 1867, 8 percent in 1890, and 9 percent in 1900.

In contrast to the creative reforms in the area of positive workman's protection in the 1880s, the negative Austrian policy towards the workers until the beginning of the 1890s was characterized by a remarkable degree of historical continuity, specifically in its continuance of a preconstitutional repression by police action and by its determination to deny the wage workers the vote. Consequently, governmental practice exhibited only a gradual shift from that prevailing during the prosperous period before the stock market crash of 1873 and the chain of grim years which followed, during which the classes and the national groups that had been shortchanged under the rule of the German liberals went over to a more intensive struggle against economic and political liberalism. This was the beginning of that great shift in party relationships as a result of which an entirely new situation had already been created in imperial Germany by 1878.

As a result of the liberal constitutional reforms of December 1867, above all of the firm establishment of basic rights, the workers' movement acquired considerable if inconsistent impetus, taking the form of workers' education associations for the most part and strongly influenced by concepts of social democracy. This development found expression in mass demonstrations such as had not been experienced in central Europe since 1848. As early as 1870 the industrial proletariat succeeded in winning for itself the right to unionize and, at least on paper, the right to strike within certain legal limitations. At the same time the late 1860s experienced a reaction from above in the form of police tricks, prohibitions [of meetings], arrests, dissolution of "politically dangerous" workers' associations, and prosecutions for treason.

Measures of this kind were simply an introduction to that policy of forceful suppression of workers' organizations demanded by the upper middle class as "the maintenance of order" and supported by the German liberals. The policy was based on the concept of government as simply a "night watchman," an idea already derided by Lassalle. In practice, the police and the police courts were entrusted with the solution of the "social question." This policy of repression was more rigorously applied after the uprising of the Paris commune and became unbending during the workers' unrest which accompanied the cyclical low of the years 1873 to 1878. . . .

In contrast to the situation in imperial Germany, the long downswing of the business cycle [in Austria] was accompanied by a retreat of the social democratic workers' movement, a virtual collapse which was only reversed by renewed growth after the reunification of the party in 1889, a permanent and deeply rooted upward movement that was contemporary with a new upswing in the business cycle beginning in the 1890s. . . .

It was indicative of Austria's economic development, not to speak of that of the much more backward Hungarian half of the empire, that the industrialization process in the period from 1879 to 1896, despite noteworthy advances in individual branches such as railroad construction, coal, iron, and cotton textiles, never got beyond the consolidation of the introductory phase, and thus remained far behind the expansion of imperial Germany. . . . [In comparison with Germany] the relative backwardness of Austrian industry and society at the end of the Great Depression was more clearly to be seen than at the high point of the long cyclical upswing in 1873. . . .

In Austria the negative resistance to the workers' struggle for greater recognition went so far that the workers' constitutional rights were practically suspended, the constitutional status quo ante 1867 was frozen in, and consequently the pretentious wage earners were refused political rights. . . . Only in 1896 did the Austrian worker, in common with other underprivileged classes—the servant remained excluded—acquire a class suffrage through the creation of a "fifth curia" for the Reichsrat. This body, however, had never had, since the adoption of constitutional methods, the true character of a popular representative body, it remained rather a kind of corporative Estates General based on hierarchical electoral privileges, an elite political and parliamentary representation of social and political interest groups. Assuredly, the reform of the voter registration system in 1882 gave the lower-middle-class and peasant possessors of property electoral status next to the aristocratic owners of estates, the rich merchants, factory owners, and bankers and the affluent cultural elite and thus allowed them to exercise a significant political influence in parliament.

That the backwardness of Austria—compared to imperial Germany—in economic development, in political institutions, in numerical strength [of the workers], and in the unequal position in public life of the preindustrial and industrial wage earners did not necessarily mean a similar underdevelopment in the area of social reform becomes clear when one looks at the positive program of the Austrian government with respect to the workers during the Great Depression. This program, as will be explained, was uncommonly progressive in the area of workmen's protection and was far more extensive in its content than what was even being talked about, let alone achieved, in Bismarck's Germany. But in the matter of political direction Austrian social policy is sharply differentiated from the course of development in Bismarckian Germany.

In Austria the emphasis was not on the further development of governmental assistance for the poor. In the course of the long cyclical downswing, the imitation of Bismarck's compulsory insurance program against the danger of impoverishment through disability remained limited to sickness and accident insurance, and in its application this program remained more limited, socially, than in Germany. The contrast lay rather, and was thereby so much the more significant in comparison with other European lands, in the positive policy of intervention taken up by the bureaucracy, in league with the Slavic and German-clerical majority in parliament. This policy aimed at insuring the worker against excessive exploitation by restricting the freedom of the employer and the foreman through relatively broad legal regulation of working conditions in middle- and large-scale industry.

The emergence of such positive concepts of social reform, and their application in Austria in legislation and administration, benefited primarily the industrial proletariat and the numerically strong group of independent small businessmen. Significantly, this "protection of the nation's work" and the collective "solidarity protectionism" did not extend to the wage earners of the preindustrial society. Messengers, daily wage workers, handicraft employees, apprentices, store clerks, as well as those industrially employed at home and farm workers remained at the mercy of their employers. In this area the unmercifully individualistic economic liberalism of the strong remained in control in practice, even if it was often elegantly dressed up with notions that stemmed from Catholic social ethics. For the poor and the dependent members of the lowest social classes, for whom the rise to the status of industrial worker was not possible, the imperceptible if experimental adoption of a "social market economy" was not mere theory: for them there was no possibility of collective self-help or of help from the state.

The progressive industrial ordinances of 1883 and 1885 for the workers in middle-sized and large enterprises formed the reverse side of the regressive protection of master craftsmen and small store owners, a kind of bipolar legislation which fitted the nature of the new Austrian social policy. In imperial Germany the small businessmen, since 1848 politically active, had succeeded in impressing the public with their loud, moving, often hysterically overplayed complaints about the oppressive power of "mobile capital," the often purely imaginary competition and price-pressure of factory industry, not to speak of the indecent competition of house-to-house salesmen. In just the same way the retail trade [in Austria], scarcely anywhere organized into large-scale undertakings, clamored for legal restrictions on "profiteers" as well as on free competition in the name of "protection of the weak". These were representatives of the traditional society who as a result of industrialization were in some cases endangered in their traditional position, but who were often inspired to new endeavor, as for instance the group of industrial workers employed at home, a group which grew rapidly in numbers between 1873 and 1896: the piece workers, the domestic craftsmen, the women and children employed at home, whose employers discovered that this type of employment offered them smaller risk, lower costs, and higher profits than factory production. After persistent agitation, strengthened by the acquisition of the suffrage in 1882, the small businessmen won for themselves legal restrictions on business and commercial freedom, open competition, and free labor contracts through the reestablishment of a guild system and the so-called "proof of competence" in the revision of the Austrian commercial law in 1883 and 1885. Additional measures, such as not extending the workmen's protection laws to small business, added to the victory.

Even in "domestic" or "cottage" industry, where under the general direction of a capitalistic entrepreneur, production actually took place in small workshops or in the homes of the workers, the workmen's protection laws were not applied. In this area, as a result, there was no legal regulation of women's and children's employment, no legally imposed restriction on hours of work, no accident insurance, and so on. Handwork was to be protected and helped to retain its competitive capability where this in fact no longer existed through the restrictions on the freedom of the [larger factory] employer and through increased costs for the medium-sized and large enterprises, as well as through tax policy, which unfairly burdened large industrial producers.

The laws for the protection of workers, particularly the new regulations for industry in 1883 and 1885, whose uncommonly progressive character was probably exceeded only by that of the Swiss legislation in this field, forbade work on Sundays and holidays as well as the truck system in all industrial-type undertakings, that is, all those employing more than twenty persons. The normal workday was limited to a maximum of 11 hours, during which breaks amounting to at least 1.5 hours had to occur. Employment of women and children was very restricted, and health protection was notably improved. These regulations were enforced by governmental inspectors, and there were additional work rules and requirements in all firms with more than twenty employees which were also subject to detailed public control. In 1883 there were 20,037 firms falling into this category in Austria this side of the Leitha. In 1891 the "reactionary" Austrian government went so far as to bring in a bill requiring the election on democratic principles of workers' councils in industrial enterprises. These councils should have a share in the administration of the various welfare arrangements as well as encourage cooperation between employer and employee in supervising adherence to the wage agreements and the working rules.

As in Germany, so in Austria social reform was a product of a suddenly emerging, manifold, pluralistic opposition to the rise of economic and political liberalism as it had developed during the prosperous period of 1849 to 1873. This opposition was a consequence of the cyclical downturn which began in 1873. The dissatisfaction, concern, even hysteria, the search for security and protection against visible dangers unleashed by the economic crisis led in Austria as in Germany to a reorientation of economic and social classes, to a shift of political forces which led in 1878–1879 to breaking the political dominance of the liberals. . . . Within Austrian society the elements that were linked socially with liberalism were in a much weaker position numerically than the corresponding elements in imperial Germany. Consequently the antiliberal protest movement found a relatively much broader social response among the nationalities of the Habsburg Empire, especially as liberalism was identified in the popular mind with the German-Jewish possessors and cultured groups and with their egotistical pursuit of their own interests.

There was, however, an even more important difference. Although different in degree, politically and socially, the antiliberal movement in Austria, seen in its totality, especially as it developed during the long cyclical downturn, was generally much more extreme in thought, radical in its assertions and goals, and often more unlimited and contradictory in its methods than its counterpart in imperial Germany. Ideologically this movement turned even more decisively against the resulting economic shift, against the new, or seemingly new, economic system as such, not merely against the previous economic policy now regarded as false, or against cyclical or personal aberrations or inadequacies. It responded, if one disregards in this connection the more progressive Social Democratic protest movement, to the unfolding of modern industrial and financial capitalism and the approaching collapse of the class-oriented, agrarian, small-business-directed, hierarchical, and aristocratic social structure with fundamental disapproval and bitter resentment. The movement therefore played much more seriously than was the case in imperial Germany with the notion of turning back the wheel of history. . . . The reaction in Austria, where the high aristocrats with large-scale, capitalistically organized agricultural holdings played a major role, was not only antiliberal, antisocialist, and anti-Semitic, it was decidedly anticapitalistic, especially with regard to industrial entrepreneurs, possessors of capital, bankers, stockbrokers, and large merchants. . . .

The early industrialization and the revolution in transport in the capital-poor Habsburg Empire—the most important industrial districts lay in lower Austria, the Steiermark, and the Bohemian-Moravian Sudetenland—were with the cooperation of foreign, especially French, participants chiefly the work of the creative initiative of German-Austrian middle-class entrepreneurs and of the Jewish financial world, which had a virtual monopoly in banking. This state of affairs explains to a considerable extent the fact that the antiliberal and anti-industrial-capital reactionary movement, which dominated politically and in parliament after 1878, acquired through the accession of the disappointed, the sobered, the anxiety-ridden, and the embittered and helpless the necessary public support and became not merely antibourgeois and anti-Semitic but in many respects also anti-German. . . . The economic crisis, whose impact varied from region to region and from class to class, had a destructive effect on the political leadership and the prestige of the Austrian Germans. The facade of a united front of all Germans collapsed altogether; and the Slavic nationalities, especially the Poles and the Czechs, increased their political activity and rose in political importance.

The government of Count Taaffe (1879–1893) was characteristic of the politics of the Great Depression. It symbolized the shift of political forces which grew out of the economic decline of 1873 to 1878. . . . After the reduction of the suffrage limitations in the reform of 1882, the parties of the "Iron Ring"—like the German liberals of the Opposition, they were [really] predemocratic parties of dignitaries—saw themselves faced with a situation of rapidly growing complexity pointing toward a radical change in the political picture: the "revolt of the masses," with its incalculable political possibilities, but also its dangers. . . . Even though the electoral reform of 1882 still denied the vote to the working classes in the cities and the country, they provided a tempting and real addition to the broadening social basis of the antiliberal movement, which received important additional impetus from the conversion of petit-bourgeois and peasant interests, which did possess the vote, into organized political action groups. This change, in the shadow of the Great Depression, revived political initiative from below as well as from above, embittered the nationalities conflict, intensified political competition, and increased political and ideological differentiation.

Within the framework of this process politicized "plebeian groups" gained ground, especially under the leadership of important organizers who pointed the way to the future and understood how to mobilize the "little man" and the educated, but unpropertied, classes. In Austria the 1880s were the founding era of the mass movements which aimed at social and political equality, material betterment, and active participation in the affairs of state. . . .

The clerical-conservative representatives of the upper aristocracy saw themselves faced with a paradoxical dilemma in the 1880s. Their own political and social-class interests, insofar as they perceived them, as well as the ideas which attracted them and in which they believed, pushed them back into a romanticized, medieval world threatened with death. Practical social and economic requirements of the present, however, drove them onward and pulled them into the witches' brew of the modern industrial society. . . . Thus the pseudodemocratic social reform rested on a false political calculation, [namely that] through substantial concessions both the Christian Democratic as well as the Social Democratic drives [for power] could be outbid. This tactical objective was linked to the illusionary expectation that in this way the movements of the urban small businessmen and industrial workers toward self-determination and political emancipation could be halted and neutralized, perhaps even converted into an obedient and satisfied collection of followers of the old social hierarchy in their battle to maintain themselves against the usurping and hated liberal-capitalistic German-Jewish plutocracy. . . .

[But] the antiliberal lower middle class, economically reactionary but politically democratized, found emotional satisfaction, a political and economic homeland, and true representation of its material interests chiefly among the Christian Socialists. The attempt of the

aristocratic social conservatives to turn the lower-middle-class movement, called into being by the Great Depression, into a traditional
self-conscious class of craftsmen succeeded only in appearance, not
in actuality, for a new spirit had been breathed into the old forms, the
spirit of a modern political mass-movement with fascistic overtones.

Karl Renner
SOCIALIST POSSIBILITIES

*Karl Renner (1870–1950), member of the Austrian Socialist party since the last
decade of the nineteenth century and one of its leaders since 1907, was from
the beginning an ardent advocate of Austrian renewal. A distinguished career
in politics—he served as chancellor of Austria and led the Austrian delegation
to the peace conference in the years immediately following World War
I—culminated in his election as president of the reconstituted Austrian Republic
after World War II. One of the leading Austrian Socialist theorists, Renner
devoted not a few of his numerous works, such as Österreich und seine
Erneuerung, which appeared in three volumes in 1916–1917, to the question of
an effective multinational system of government. The following selection is
from a posthumous work,* Die Nation: Mythos und Wirklichkeit. *Renner's
analysis is given added urgency by his awareness of the catastrophic effects of
unrestrained nationalism in central and eastern Europe, culminating in World
War II.*

Every struggle of the nationalities in a state of mixed nationalities
reveals itself . . . as a battle over the [control of the] government,
which is parallel in its nature to the struggle of the large single
nationality for its own national state. Without participating in the
sovereign rights of government, the nation, the community of speech
and culture, cannot flourish, cannot even maintain itself. The nationality demands recognition for its tongue in school and public office, and
without this recognition the tongue sinks [rapidly] to a simple dialect.
National culture always rests in great part on governmental institutions, without them it degenerates. Public service claims an important

From Karl Renner, *Die Nation: Mythos und Wirklichkeit* (Vienna, Cologne, Stuttgart,
Zürich, 1964), pp. 93–99, 103–105. Translated by permission of Europa Verlag A.G.

part of the national community, and without being able to train this segment [of the nationality] in its own high schools and universities and to give them daily tests in practical service, the nationality remains merely rudimentary [in its development]. The economy, which appears to the superficial observer to be independent of national distinctions, requires, in the nation-state era in which we live and in which the government so extensively affects economic life, the encouragement of the public authorities. If this is denied the minority, it also degenerates economically. If the minority has to give up its claim to the recognition of its tongue, then it only takes one to two generations before its members as individuals switch their tongues, are recognized by the other [politically recognized] nation, and work their way up in it. (The immigrants in the United States [are a good example].) Until their children are assimilated, the minority experiences all the deprivations and humiliations which foreigners necessarily have to suffer.

The struggle of the nations . . . therefore, is recapitulated in a more modern form and under changed conditions within the boundaries of every single land of mixed nationalities. Here, to be sure, the ethnic groups find themselves in the unfortunate situation that the authority of the state, at first united, cannot become a power instrument of each of them right from the beginning. Therefore the central issue of all struggles is possession of a part of this governmental authority, whether it be a portion that can be geographically segregated or an area that is functionally separable, whether a province or a ministry, the presidency of a province, or merely a secretarial post.

The war among nation-states with deadly weapons is a mighty, yet chronologically limited, struggle. Victory and defeat can both, under [certain] circumstances, have a fruitful, liberating effect. Such methods of sheer physical power are—generally at least—out of the question in a land of mixed nationalities; here the struggle [among the nationalities] extends in exhausting continuity through decades, even through centuries.

These struggles pit not merely one nationality against another, but simultaneously each nationality against the central power which is to be found, before the nationality itself becomes historically conscious, in the hands of the local princes, of the directing and administering bureaucracy, and of the army. The struggle first makes its appearance as a respectful and enviable competition of the ethnic groups for the favor of the head of the dynasty and his aides, but also at times, should this favor change or be withheld, as a wild rebellion against the traditional bearers of the authority of the state.

The traditional government, however, from monarch down to the gendarme, prefers to ignore for as long as possible the task that is set for it and is glad of the opportunity to play one group off against another. The government distinguishes merely between rulers and ruled, for a long time it regards the nationality question merely as the technical problem of adapting the administration to the uncomfortable fact that within the area of its authority persons using different spoken tongues exist who should be obliged and justified in conceding and recognizing rights of speech. The government starts out, therefore, with the relationship of individual to state and denies that the nationality is a collective entity desiring to be incorporated as such into the state. It rejects the notion of conceding to the ethnic groups as large official interest blocs specific influence on legislation, administration, and justice, thus limiting the power of the prince and of his bureaucracy and eventually arrives at the legal loophole of establishing the preservation of the national tongue and other distinctive national qualities as a mere subjective civil right of the individual. All the constitutions of Austria from the year 1849 to the downfall of the empire start from this basis of the civil rights of the individual in relation to one, undifferentiated, centralistic state authority.

The word nationality, which in the Latin lands means citizenship, henceforth takes on [in lands of mixed nationalities] a specific legal meaning: it designates the subjective quality of a citizen, insofar as he speaks a definite language as mother tongue or in daily usage. This quality is conceded case by case, not in the fashion of birthplace or religious affiliation legally and officially, but it is legally relevant: the citizen has the right to claim his own rights and to acknowledge those of others in this tongue. The nationality problem appears to limit itself to the question of schools and public offices. This subjective qualification underlies school laws and requirements as to official languages.

The nations of Austria were happy at this first success but accepted it without any special thanks, [for] they harbored far more extensive demands.

Nationality propaganda very soon advanced the proposition that the land of mixed nationalities was not merely an inorganic heaping up of individuals having different tongues, but that the nationalities in

FIGURE 6. "Gentlemen, the hazelnuts and rubber bands will now be distributed. We can then begin right away with the special debate!" *(Cartoon by Bruno Paul,* Simplicissimus *6 JHRG. No. 51 (1901))*

their collective being ought to be regarded as the units that form the [central] government. The increased self-consciousness of the nationality also claims for itself the right of a special community existence, it wants to see the individual first integrated into the nationality and then through this indirectly into the [central] government. The multinational state appears to the nationality as a union of nations, not as the centralization of individuals. In the older, centralistic conception [of the relationship of individual to government] the nationality question arises as a question of languages and offices, that is in the main as a technical administrative question, but for the ideology of self-conscious nationalism the matter is one of the whole organization of the government, that is, a constitutional question.

Thus the nationality, legally regarded, wants to become a collective legal personality, even in those places where it lacks the power to reach out for the diadem of sovereignty: it demands instead of full sovereignty that recognized independent share of governmental power designated by the word "autonomy." The struggle for autonomy in different lands and in different phases of their history varies—not least in relation to the size and persistence of the minority—in several ways and creates a variegated, confusing pattern of legal relationships, which henceforth should be classified as juridical.

If we take the development in old Austria, which in this respect had gone farthest, as an example, the following divergences are to be found: first, as to the way in which the mass of the individual members of the nationality should be brought together into a single entity (the organizational principle); second, as to the extent of the legal rights with which the nationality as organized entity should be endowed (the juridical issue); thirdly, as to the way in which the nationalities should be related to the central government (the manner of federation). All three of these issues, which should be carefully dissociated from minority right as such and which will later be discussed in greater detail, derive from one key issue: how is the national tie formed *legally,* and is it legally distinguished from other social groupings? We propose to consider this question first.

In accordance with the pattern of the sovereign national states in the vicinity, the partial or splinter nationality inside a multinational state views the bond of the populace—in accordance with the high significance the [inhabited] area always has for the life of the whole nation—with the area it has always inhabited as the decisive fact, the nationality views itself first and foremost as a community of settlers. This, the sacrosanct homeland, the "land of our forefathers," constitutes the substratum which is to become a legal institution. Thence the national longing to see the nation [recognized] legally as a territorial union and, therefore, to see it constituted as a territorial body. In the form of autonomous provinces with increased self-government, in which the administration and the schools preserve the national tongue and only members of the nationality can occupy public office, the nationality shall pursue its own life. At that point where the nationalities are clearly divided from one another, or even where the province is the remnant of an earlier independent political entity later incorporated into a larger whole, as for example Bohemia into old Austria, the demand for the re-creation of historic political rights appears (historical delimitation). The historical dress in which the national demand is draped, the "yellowed documents" which should support it, covers an entirely modern striving towards the future. It is [in fact] not a question of the province and its old, medieval rights, but [rather] of the basic requirements of the nationality for its [future] development.

At that point where the national settlement area is to be sure clearly defined, but is not coterminous with such historic boundaries, as for example the case of the Slovenes in old Austria, the minority demands in most cases a totally new definition of the [national] territory: this was the case in Austria in the Kremsier Assembly of 1849. Nonhistoric nations, which for the first time develop a political life or first reawaken after a long time, naturally tend to favor this "ethnic" delimitation.

[But] the territorial approach doesn't always lead to the goal, whether it is "historic" or "ethnic." In some cases, especially in eastern Europe, the original settlement took place in such a way as to make a territorial delimitation ridiculous. The whole of the Danube Valley, as well as the area east of the Oder [River], shows us an ethnographic map with many extrusions and enclaves, scattered settlements, and a mosaiclike network of small groups speaking different tongues which lacks all rhyme and reason. In the smallest of the original provinces of old Austria, the Bukovina, four nationalities lived together, and yet, as we shall see, the public law of this land was able to adapt to this confusing situation in ideal fashion. In such cases, territorial delimitation is impossible, because, from the practical, administrative point of view the result is a division into minute particles.

This unfortunate heritage of historic mixing of ethnic groups has been made even more complicated in the most recent period of industrial development: large cities have arisen at communications centers, and not infrequently (Brussels [is a good example]) precisely on the linguistic border, that draw immigrants from both ethnic groups and thoroughly mix them up within the borders of the city. In similar fashion industrial districts, even when they were originally wholly contained within the area occupied by one nationality, draw immigrants from considerable distances and create within their boundaries a mixture which cannot be untangled. Such developments have produced total confusion in the linguistic map of old Austria. For such cases absolutism and its bureaucracy produced the solution of "simultaneous languages" in school and public office. The nationalistic ideology protested against such solutions because they cut public office and school, official and teacher, off from the influence of the nationality and made them, in its words, "nationally sexless."

Another form of delimitation emerged, another way of thinking [about this problem]: in view of the many internal migrations, of the mixing up of the ethnic groups in a given area, of the freedom to come and go and the modern forms of transportation that separated men from their ancestral plots and brought people of very different ethnic origins together in places far distant from their original homes, the organization of nationalities in multinational states on the basis of fixed territorial boundaries appeared hopeless. Wasn't the residence of the moment in fact, in terms of national self-consciousness, always secondary? Why not treat the nation legally as a kind of union of persons, as a society of individuals, such as had for years been done in the case of religious affiliations? The idea of *personal autonomy* gained ground. Shortly before the war in the most ethnically mixed lands of old Austria, Moravia and the Bukovina, this idea was adopted legally, and it underlay the unrealized project of a constitution for Bosnia and Herzegovina. Something quite new appeared to have been created both in law and in fact—and yet it merely mirrored that which the Saxons of the Siebenbürgen had adopted many centuries before in their "university of the nations."

This personal delimitation [of ethnic ties] presupposes that membership in the nation, the nationality, is not merely a technical qualification of the individual according to his language of preference, but that it is legally established through a "declaration of national affiliation" and confirmed by enrollment in a "national cadaster"—a special list of the citizens of each nationality, so that the membership in such a nationality becomes in fact a semiofficial group or organization with legally recognized status; such nationalities are constituted in appropriate constitutional fashion through elections and thus the nation is created as the possessor of public and private rights, and the nation as a group takes part in legislation and administration. *Thus instead of the community of settlement the community of culture which is the nation becomes the basis of legal institutions,* and minority rights are built up on this basis. The legislative bodies (the provincial legislatures of old Austria, for example) are divided up into *national curias,* the administration into national sections; public authority appears, insofar as special national interests come into it, to be not territorially but functionally divided; but in all cases where the common, supranational interests of the state are to be preserved this public authority is again brought together in a federally organized government. In cities of mixed ethnic composition in old Austria, there could be found historic models of a most interesting sort [for this kind of constitutional structure].

Only such a system can create a legal existence for the ethnic minority; it can possess property and can satisfy the interests of the community through provisions of its own. The first step is the creation of national communities in those cities and towns of mixed ethnic make-up. It is the simplest conceivable administrative task to construct lists of citizens separated into their national affiliation, so-called national cadasters. Once such national communities have been created, all higher-level development of community life can follow from these without further difficulty. . . .

For the network of middle positions in the governmental administration, which exist under such names as provinces, lands, districts, and the like, historical necessities are far more restricting than in the case of local offices. In an earlier era the largely sovereign provincial rulers created provincial capitals, where the princely residence, barracks, government office buildings, and the centers of higher education are concentrated. This inheritance has been magnified in capitalistic and middle-class circles by the centralization of railroad, postal, and telegraph installations in the provincial capital. In the beginnings of the era of capitalistic development (more or less from 1848 to 1870), the division of such lands according to the territorial principle was not yet terribly difficult, but it proved with passing decades ever more complicated. Absolute governments also resisted division at this level and preferred to fence in two or more nationalities within one province, to let them work off their energies in competition with one another, and thus to be able to play off one against another. A thoroughgoing division into departments, such as that in France in

1789, could have occurred in Austria only as a result of revolution; it was attempted in Czechoslovakia immediately after the founding of that state in 1919 but was later abandoned in favor of the historic division into provinces.

No matter how the middle-level administration is formed, national self-government is only possible when democratic popular representation, rather than a bureaucratic central authority, controls the administration. In every multinational state a number of one-language, a number of two-language, and possibly here and there three-language provinces will exist. Legislation and administration are effected, as already explained, in part in common in all purely economic and social matters, in part through curias and sections in national cultural questions. Curias and sections have civil and legal status.

The last step is the fusion of the nationalities into a single whole and their incorporation into the government for the whole country. After the breakup of Austria[-Hungary] the nationalities in practice fulfilled the first task: the representatives of all parts of a nationality, whether elected in areas where that nationality was in the majority or where it was in the minority, joined together to form an assembly of the nations (the Germans of Austria formed a national assembly), and this supreme authority of the nationality immediately took on governmental functions. Had the Habsburg government embarked on this step before the war, the empire might be standing today. Most assuredly, the second step was never carried through because the victorious powers [of World War I] decided on the breakup of Austria-Hungary and the founding of sovereign successor states—as I maintain, to the disadvantage of all participants and to the detriment of all Europe; but the second step necessary for the maintenance of the empire was determined by the nature of things as well as by the results of the struggles of a century: next to an imperial representative body based on universal suffrage a house of nationalities would have existed as upper house [of the imperial legislature], which was to be formed from the delegates of all the national groups. This is the necessary linkage of the parts to the whole, that which earlier was designated "federative."

[Thus] the multinational state is not merely in fact but also in law a condominium of several nations, the earlier unitary state is turned into a federation: the union of nationalities is the ideal governmental form for such ethnically mixed areas. Austria's Social Democratic party adopted this goal at the Convention in Brünn in 1899 as the common program of the proletariat of all the nations of the old empire.

Austria was caught by surprise by the World War as she was halfway toward the achievement of this goal, and she was destroyed before a truly international legal structure, which was in process of developing, could be fully realized within the boundaries of this one state. In the process many extremely interesting and original legal innovations, of which the outside world and especially the world of the victorious Allies of World War I knew scarcely anything, were partially or totally destroyed. They had enjoyed a lively existence for some years and had proved their potentiality and practical worth.

Karl Kautzky
SOCIALIST REALITIES

Karl Kautzky (1854—1938), himself of Czech extraction, had already joined the Socialist party while he was a student in Vienna. By profession a journalist, he is most widely known as the author of many theoretical expositions of the Socialist position, not the least of these the famous Erfurt Program of 1891 of the German Social Democratic party. He served five years as private secretary to Friedrich Engels. In the many battles within the Socialist movement, Kautzky took up a middle position, rejecting revisionism on the right, syndicalism and pure bolshevism on the left. In his old age he returned to Vienna to live. The following selection reveals his intimate personal knowledge of the nationality conflicts of the Austrian Empire, which he seeks to relate to the developing Socialist movement.

Russia is a cross between national state and multinational state. The latter finds its classic form only where, among several nations in a state, none towers so high over the others that it can by means of its sheer superiority, without any political pressure, become the dominant nationality [controlling the state].

Among the true multinational states (nationality states) one must further distinguish between those with only two and those with several nationalities.

From Karl Kautzky, *Die Vereinigten Staaten Mitteleuropas* (Stuttgart, 1916), pp. 32–49. Translated by permission of Verlag J. H. Dietz Nachfolger G.m.b.H.

The nationality problem is much simpler for the first [group]. It is then sufficient that, together with wide national freedom and local self-administration, in place of an official language two coequal languages [can] be accepted in the administration and legislation of the government, in order to eliminate most of the difficulties caused by language differences. This [arrangement] will be further promoted where one of the two languages is a world language whose acquisition has more than local advantages and therefore is not considered an intolerable burden.

In 1910 in Belgium 2,833,334 inhabitants spoke only French, 3,220,662 only Flemish, and 871,288 were masters of both languages.

The position of Switzerland as a multinational state is unique. It is made easier by the wide areas of cantonal sovereignty. Four languages are spoken there, but two of these are in such a decisively advantageous position because of the number who speak both or even one of them, that they can be considered as official languages: German and French. Italian plays only a subsidiary role. It is only spoken by a large portion of the population in two of the twenty-five cantons. Romansh [is spoken] only in one canton and then only by a minority.

Far more complicated are the relationships in Austria, a multinational state unlike any other in Europe. It is inhabited by nine nations, including four large ones, of which none towers so far above the others that its numbers alone give it an obvious and generally recognized superiority. So we find united in this state 12 million Germans, 10 million Hungarians, 8.5 million Czechs and Slovaks, 6.5 million Serbocroatians, or, if one joins the Slovenes to them, more than 7.5 million South Slavs. Besides these there are still to be considered 5 million Poles, 4 million Ruthenians (Little Russians), and 3.5 million Rumanians. For a long time the Germans functioned in this conglomerate as the politically dominant nationality. [Then] however, the rulers of the Habsburg hereditary lands were German emperors, the Germans [were] the economic and intellectually developed nationality, [and] German was not only the language of the bureaucracy and the army but also the normal language of the educated. When, however, the ties of Austria to the German Reich ended at the same time that capitalism spread among the other nationalities, the superiority of the Germans was undermined. They hoped to maintain themselves as dominant nationality in the western half of the empire, if they left the eastern [half] to the Magyars. They thereby abandoned 2 million Germans in Hungary to the Magyar hegemony. Also divided in this cause were the Czechoslovaks, of whom 2 million lived in Hungarian areas. Most peculiar and confused was the legal position of the Serbocroatians. A portion came directly [under] Hungarian [rule], a portion [became] Austrian, and a third [portion] in Croatia occupied a special position within the Hungarian state. A further special position was accorded to a fourth part in Bosnia.

The legal confusion reflected the confusion of the national aims of the various peoples. Some of them border on independent, in some cases blooming and powerful states of the same nationality. For example, Rumanians, Serbians, Italians, and Germans. This arouses in them desires and wishes which strike across the border but not in the same manner in each case. The nationally inclined Germans indeed feel a strong attraction for the German Reich, but, on the other hand, the claim to function as the dominant political nationality [in Austria] directs their aspirations more towards the east and south. The formation of [a] Central Europe[an Federation] seems to them to be the proper means to enable them to unite these two opposing tendencies in a higher synthesis.

Quite different are the tendencies of the Poles and Ruthenians. They also have the largest portion of their national fellows across the frontiers. However, as yet, they are not united in separate, independent national states but are included in [other] great powers as minorities. Their national aspirations reveal, therefore, especially in the case of the Poles, a tendency hostile to the neighboring state.

Only two of the nations fall completely within the limits of the monarchy, the Hungarians and the Czechs. In both we find a high degree of national consciousness, although both are nonetheless strongly interested in the existence of Austria. Not, however, because the age of world economy no longer tolerates small national states. That is, as we have seen, a completely unfounded assumption. On the other hand, [they desire the continuation of Austria] because in this age a state lacks light and air when it is denied access to the open seas. The open seas are the only free road which, in peacetime, any state can travel unhindered. A state that has access to the world ocean therefore has access to the world market. The freedom of the seas in times of peace does not have to be fought for; it is a firmly established fact. Anyone who makes the freedom of the seas a war aim is not thinking of the coming peace but of the next war. It is often only a different way of demanding the destruction of English seapower.

On the other hand, a state which has no access to the open seas is fully dependent upon its neighbors even in peacetime, [at the mercy of] their tariff and railway policy. Such a state can suffer seriously if superior powers are its neighbors and hamstring its world trade. Not the freedom of the seas, but access to the seas is a vital consideration for every state involved in capitalistic production. Serbia has learned this the hard way.

It is no accident that with one exception the viable and blooming small states of Europe all lie on the sea: the three Scandinavian states, Holland, and Belgium. Switzerland is the single exception. She has the good fortune to be surrounded by four neighbors with such disparate interests that she can be certain the moment will never come when all four conspire against her. One way or another the road to the sea will always remain open to her. Even so her geographic location, but not her small size, is definitely an unfavorable factor in the maintenance of her economic independence. . . .

An independent Czech national state, like a Hungarian one, would be cut off from the sea, despite Shakespeare, who granted Moravia a seacoast. Fiume does not lie in a Hungarian but in a Serbo-Croatian language area. Both national states would therefore be in desperate straits. This [situation] gives both the Magyars and the Czechs a considerable interest in the survival of Austria-Hungary despite their strong national drive. But even in their case, this interest asserts itself in diverse and contradictory ways. For the Hungarians are the ruling nationality and wish to retain this position. The Czechs wish to achieve full political equality; their hotspurs indeed feel that it is the right of their nation to become a ruling nation. They stand in opposition to the Germans and Hungarians.

None of the nations has such a preponderance over the others that it can dominate the central government. Each is dependent for the achievement of specific goals upon the support of one of the other nations which agrees with it on that point but does not follow the same general policy regarding the government as a whole. Therefore, up to now, every unified, consistent regulation of the national relationships on the basis of principle has been thwarted. All actions in this sphere have been undertaken case by case in limited areas with countless reservations, [so that] each solution of a portion of the problem only created new problems. The only consistently followed method was that of "muddling through"; each achievement in the national sphere meant only a [further] complication of the national relationships.

Comrade Renner has worked out a very clever plan by which the national relationships of Austria are to be satisfactorily resolved. It is in its way as ingenious as Fourier's planned *Phalanstère*. But the millionaire to provide the money for the realization of his plans for whom he [Fourier] waited never came. And also to date there is no sign of a power which is capable of and willing to carry out the Renner plan. After the [First World] War we will see if anything has changed as a result of the conflict.

Doubtless an Austria organized on Renner's lines would be as pleasant a community as Fourier's *Phalanstère*. It could indeed tower above the existing national states [and] appear in contrast to them as a higher form of political organization.

But here we are dealing, not with plans, hopes, and expectations, but with the experiences of history to date, and these show us no multinational state equal to a national state in internal power. They show us problems and difficulties in multinational states which national states never encounter. And, finally, they show us not the least tendency toward unification of the existing national states with developed political life of the masses into international world powers.

The tendency demonstrated by our epoch toward the unification of various groups of peoples into a world power is expressed only in the annexation of areas remaining politically without rights by means of colonial policy. Wherever we find various nations with a developed political life of the masses united in a common system, it is only their national life which is a result of recent history, not, however, their unification. This is a matter of much older history, a carry-over from the past, not the kernel of a new future.

The single exception is the annexation of the Boer Republics by the British Empire. This exception took place in Africa and is a side effect of colonial policy. In Europe recent decades have given us no example of a lasting union of different national states into a common community, but only two developments in the opposite direction: the splitting of Austria into two states, one of which, the Hungarian, has succeeded in achieving autonomy; and the dissolution of the union between Sweden and Norway. The latter development transformed a federal state of 7 million inhabitants into two small national states, one of which has over 5 and the other over 2 million inhabitants.

This event, which took place ten years ago, clearly disproves the alleged effeteness of the national state and its decline in favor of the international federation of states.

The course of development which the creation of a Central Europe is [supposed] to promote exists only in the imaginations of the proponents of this plan. . . .

Our examination of the prospects of Central Europe would be incomplete were it to remain entirely negative and critical. We have demonstrated that the modern development of the state is not toward the transformation of the national state into a supranational giant state. This does not by any means indicate that all of the individual classes which have until now striven toward the national state still hold fast to this goal today and that the national idea has remained undisturbed by the transformation of the classes brought about by the gigantic developments of the past decades. How do the individual classes stand today with regard to the national idea?

Scarcely twenty years ago, in January 1898, [I] published in the *Neue Zeit* an article concerning the "Conflict of Nationalities and Public Law in Austria" in which I revealed the roots of the national idea. I said there:

The modern national idea, whose rise accompanied the development of the modern state throughout Europe is not entirely a hallucination or a swindle . . . but [is] deeply rooted in the needs of the peoples. Three factors seem to us to be active in its development: first, the need of the middle class, especially the manufacturers, to secure an internal market for themselves and to expand the external one as much as possible, which led to cutting [themselves] off from outsiders and to cooperation against foreign competitors. This need can best be fulfilled by the national state. . . .

A second root of the modern national idea is the struggle for political freedom, toward democracy, whose economic imperatives we will not discuss here, but which has appeared as a powerful force in all developed states in this century. It consists of the struggle for full sovereignty of the people, which wishes to determine its own fate freely and which opposes every external force, be it a person, a class, or another nation.

We see the third root of modern national aspirations in the spread of literary, national education among the masses of the people. That is in essence a peculiar development of the nineteenth century. Heretofore we find, aside from occasional exceptions, a popular poetry and a certain popular knowledge based on oral tradition which did not rise above the local isolation of the individual villages and towns. And beside this [development] a literature which was the privilege of an aristocratic minority and was so foreign to the popular life that it was long carried on in a foreign language and had a primarily international character . . . .

The formal education of the masses became an economic necessity in the nineteenth century, and economic as well as political life forced the masses to reach an understanding with one another on the basis of larger areas and to familiarize themselves with new spheres [of learning]. Beside the book literature there arose a newspaper literature, and both penetrated into ever wider circles of the populace. In this way the smaller nations, too, developed the basis for their own literature, primarily a newspaper literature. . . .

All of these roots of the modern national movements are deeply anchored in the development of modern society.

Each of the three factors of the modern national state discussed above is characteristic of a different class. The first [is characteristic of] the capitalists, the second of the working classes, the third of the intellectuals. Each of these classes stands in a special relationship to the national idea and lends to it a special character.

The national feeling of the working classes rests at the same time on their interest in national policy—or, more correctly, it is a part of it—wherever national independence or unification faces barriers. The masses do not merely strive for democratic rights, they strive for the right to exercise them. This possibility is automatically denied to them where the language of the state and of political activity is not their language. If democracy is to become a reality, the popular language must also be the official language. This is only possible in the national state. This aim is one of the goals of democratic strivings wherever it had not been achieved before the rise of democracy.

Like so many other ideals this one also does not find complete realization everywhere. We have already seen that in some multinational states there are nationalities whose geographic position as well as historically extablished terms of existence make the realization of a nation-state very difficult. There remains for them only the surrogate of the achievement of national autonomy within the multinational state to which they have belonged. That means, however, neither the renunciation of the general tendency toward national independence nor a denial of the fact that this can only be fully achieved in the national state.

The national desires of the worker-democracy are satisfied by the achievement of national independence. What it [the working class] demands for itself as a people it is ready to concede to the democracy of every other people. Indeed, democracy here is thus reinforced greatly by [democracy] there. If democracy were achieved everywhere and the independence of peoples [were] recognized, then each would be secure in the same manner, whether it was large or small. No nation [would] need to grow at the expense of the others; none [would] threaten the other then, [so that] the age of eternal peace comes correspondingly nearer the more widely democracy is spread. . . .

The intimate ties of democracy with national independence made the absolute government of the first half of the century as active against national tendencies as against democratic ones. . . . The carriers of the democratic movement were then as now the working classes. In this category are to be included all who live from their own work, not from that of others. Among them, however, the artisans, the lower middle class, were decisive, not the proletariat. Therefore one can say that the struggle for national independence is a heritage from the lower middle class, but that is also the case with regard to democracy, the fight for the ballot, for freedom of the press, and for internationalism. The proletariat therefore, when it reached independent class consciousness and came to the class struggle, did not give up these goals but became their most vigorous champion after the lower middle classes had betrayed them and sold out to middle-class leadership. . . .

The national aspirations of the intellectuals differ from those of the classes that live by the work of their hands. In general these [intellectuals] do not form a class with sharply delineated class interests. Their members easily attach themselves to other classes whose interests they represent, capitalists as well as aristocrats and, on the other side, the lower middle class or proletarians. Thereby they share the national aspirations of the class whose struggle they support.

The more the intellectual group grows and its professions diversify themselves, the less possible it is to consider them, in all their ramifications and mutually exclusive interests, as a special class or party. What the Catholic church could still accomplish in the Middle Ages is now impossible.

However, despite all divergence of professional interests, almost all [intellectuals] with the exception of sculptors, painters, and musicians have in common the fact that language is their tool, indeed their means of production. Therefore all questions regarding language are of particular interest to them, beyond the question of democracy itself. Even where participation in the lower-middle class or proletarian struggle for democracy does not make the language question significant for them, [even] where pure self-interest moves them, language is of decisive importance for them. The market area of the intellectual, whether he is journalist or dramatist, official or lawyer, doctor or teacher, etc., is [among] those who speak his language. The more extended this market, the better his economic and social position, the greater the circle he reaches and influences. . . . Therefore the independence of his nation is not enough for him. Its size and growth are equally significant in his eyes.

The other nations, on the other hand, are more or less immaterial to him. He cannot reach them unless he achieves world renown [and] is translated into foreign languages. This is not the case with most intellectuals. He easily finds himself directly hostile to the other nations wherever the power of the state seems to offer him the possibility of broadening in this manner the area in which his own language dominates. In a multinational state, for example, this is possible by means of an appropriate structure of the school system. . . .

The national aims of the capitalists are closely related to the national and supranational aims of the intellectuals but are not identical with them. [This is] because the area of [possible] profit is not identical with the language area.

The capitalists, like the intellectuals and even the workers, are interested in the independence of their nation and in the national state. They must above all oppose being excluded from the domination of the state in which they live and have their enterprises by capitalists of other nations or even against being restrained by [such capitalists]. Where the bureaucracy limits the development of productive forces the capitalists even develop a certain interest in political freedom.

But unlike the intellectuals they do not lay the greatest stress upon having the workers belong to their nationality. For them the surplus value the worker produces is decisive, not the language he speaks. The foreign-speaking [worker] is often more welcome to them, if he is cheaper or produces greater surplus value. They demand under some circumstances the introduction of foreign workers by every possible pressure although these [workers] threaten to alter the language frontier and drive the intellectuals of their nation to despair.

The foreign worker, for example the Czech, in a mixed-language area will indeed, if he does not understand German, prefer not only the doctor and lawyer of his own nation when he needs aid, but as a consumer will also prefer to find a merchant and bar owner who speak his own tongue. On the other hand, not only the Czech doctor and lawyer, but also the Czech merchant and bar owner, in an area inhabited by Czechs and Germans will not wish to see the Czech workers learn German because then the possibility arises that they [the workers] will go over to their German competitors. In such cases, the interests of the capitalists and the intellectuals are united in opposition to those of the workers. These win, as consumers, when they can use both languages because they then have a choice among the competitors. They also win as class strugglers because they can better cooperate with their class comrades of the other nationality—to say nothing of the widening of the spiritual horizon which every man achieves by means of studying a foreign language. . . .

Once the privileged position of the capitalists and the language workers has disappeared, the national conflicts also come to an end, for there remains nothing in the need for national autonomy which can bring one nation into conflict with another. The international cooperation in intellectual and material production arising from the requirements of the modern world economy can then proceed completely unhampered toward increasingly close relationships among [all] nations.

Rudolf Wierer

WAR AND COLLAPSE

The last stages of the empire were initimately bound up with the fact of the world war. The death of the old emperor, Francis Joseph, in 1916, the accession of a new and young ruler as anxious to come to grips with the manifold problems of his inheritance as his predecessor had been in his day led to a new attempt to find solutions to the problems of the empire. Yet the time for constitutional reconstructions had evidently come and gone, if it had ever arrived. Rudolf Wierer (b. 1907), a native of Moravia who lived through the war and postwar era, shows that the conditions of war and defeat made any spontaneous effort by those who had previously determined the fate of the Danube Valley superfluous. The fate of the monarchy was more than ever before in the hands of forces over which it had no control.

The collapse of the Bulgarian front led to the gradual dissolution of Austria-Hungary. Hunger provoked isolated uprisings which demoralized the exhausted army. Consequently the emperor Charles I, through the Austrian cabinet of Hussarek, attempted a [last] reorganization of the monarchy in accordance with Wilson's Fourteen Points. Yet the majority of the representatives of the non-German Austrian nationalities—especially the Czechs and the South Slavs—rejected the government's plan to form an Austrian, Bohemian, Ukrainian, and South Slav substate; this rejection was clearly enunciated at an interview with the emperor on 12 October 1918.

In order to insure Wilson's sympathy for Austria-Hungary, the emperor finally determined to issue a manifesto, on 16 October 1918, in which he anticipated the reconstruction of Austria, according to the wishes of its nationalities, into a federal state, reserving at the express wish of the Hungarian minister-president Wekerle, the integrity of the crown of St. Stephen. Every nationality was to have in its own area its own political institutions. The possible union of the Polish areas with an independent Polish state was in no way prejudiced by this proposal, and further, the city of Triest with its surrounding territory was to enjoy a special status.

The manifesto was based on an ethnic principle of nationality,

From Rudolf Wierer, *Der Föderalismus im Donauraum* (Böhlau Verlag, Wien-Köln-Graz, 1960), pp. 153–155. Translated by permission of Verlagsbuchhandlung Hermann Böhlaus Nachfolger.

which at one time had been proposed by Charmatz for Austria, by Popovici for the entire monarchy. The legislative representatives [Reichsrat deputies] of each nationality should constitute themselves a national council and draw up rules for the mutual relations of nationality to imperial government and of the various nationalities to one another. The imperial manifesto promised to follow constitutional procedures and to offer Wilson and the Entente, as well as the individual Austrian nationalities, a guarantee that the national right to self-determination would be adhered to. At the same time it sought to insure by democratic means the preservation of the minimum necessary economic and political unity to cover common needs of the people of Austria. A proclamation of the minister-president on the same date emphasized that the change should be carried out legally and without undue pressure.

Nevertheless, the manifesto did not achieve the desired results, but merely hastened the dissolution of Austria and consequently of Austria-Hungary. The long war undermined the centripetal forces which had still exercised a powerful influence, at the beginning of the war and, under the influence of military failure, strengthened the tendency to resistance both among those who had been antagonistic toward the monarchy from the beginning, a minority, and among those who had approved of it, a majority. These two factors combined to a certain degree to produce an almost bloodless revolution, which among the non-German elements had a nationalistic character.

The complicated constitutional structure of the monarchy contributed in the moment of crisis only to weakening the forces that would have had a conservative effect in a nationally uniform state. Hungary took advantage of the manifesto, despite all of Austria's concessions, to proclaim the end of dualism and the substitution of a more personal union, quite obviously because Magyars who had formerly supported dualism feared the ideological and national infection of the non-Magyar elements in Hungary from Austria.

In Austria the manifesto met with decided opposition even from the conservative minorities in those nationalities—Czechs, Poles—which had already determined upon separation, because it rejected the absolute independence of Czechs and Poles while assuring it to the Hungarians. On the other hand, the political and psychological dissolution of Austria had already proceeded too far to win back the South Slavs and the Ukrainians through the concession of the ethnic-nationality principle for which they had so long campaigned. Thus the last Austrian "liquidation" cabinet was formed under Lammasch, assuring the dissolution of the monarchy when it determined to adopt the republican form of government on 12 November 1918.

IV THE EMPIRE IN RETROSPECT

The collapse of the Austrian Empire, forming as it did part of the collapse of the entire old order of government and society in central and eastern Europe, has attracted rather less attention than might be expected. Regarded at first merely as the fruition of Allied war aims, which were directed towards helping democracy win out over recalcitrant and anachronistic forms of political organization, the reasons for the internal failure of the empire—a failure which preceded and laid the groundwork for defeat in World War I—were at first of interest only to the Austrians themselves. World War II, an object lesson in the consequences of excessive allegiance to the principle of nationalism as the criterion of political and social order, has stirred greater interest in the whole question of the validity of the Austrian Empire, and has provoked a reevaluation of the forces operating for, as well as against, the empire.

Robert A. Kann
THE EMPIRE: VICTIM OF DISINTEGRATIVE FORCES

Robert A. Kann ranks before all other modern scholars in his intimate knowledge of the manifold problems of the Austrian Empire. This knowledge is embodied above all in his masterful and detailed two-volume work, The Multi-National Empire *(New York, 1950). Viennese by birth and a practicing lawyer in Vienna until 1938, Kann has, since coming to the United States, acquired increasing recognition as the expert on the nationality problems of the empire. The following selection is from an interpretive study by Kann on the Austrian Empire.*

The first problem for discussion here is the role of overall tradition deriving from age-old common historical experiences, forms of government and institutions. Obviously, such common experiences are likely to be more limited in the multinational state than in a national one. Nevertheless the mere existence of these common experiences and their implications on the political life of the people in the multinational state are still significant. However, the effect of these factors of common experience and tradition may in practice be more or less canceled out by the political, social and cultural practices which have grown up within the various ancient historico-political units from which the empire evolved, and, more recently by the ethnic national traditions revised and revived in the nineteenth and twentieth centuries. . . .

With regard to the specific problem of consolidation the following topics demand particular attention:

Dynasty
Armed forces
Religious affiliation
Bureaucracy
Aristocracy
Supranational party ideologies
Economic system

From *The Habsburg Empire: A Study in Integration and Disintegration* by Robert A. Kann, pp. 7–15. Copyright © 1957 by The Center for Research on World Political Institutions of Princeton University. Excerpted and reprinted by permission of Praeger Publishers, Inc., New York.

129

The first two factors listed pose the least difficult problems, and only minor reservations as to their consolidating effects are necessary. The dynasty constituted the manifest, supreme, though after 1867 weakened, unifying bond between the Habsburg lands. If one goes back in history beyond the Compromise to the Magyar War of Independence of 1849 and further to the Union of 1526–1527, one will realize, however, that the status of the dynasty in west and east was rooted in different foundations. The House of Habsburg in the German-Austrian lands—and, until the battle of the White Mountain in 1620 in the Bohemian domains as well—offered in its centers, Vienna and Prague, imperial grandeur and increasing international prestige. To outlying Hungary, on the other hand, an area for generations exposed to the Turkish onslaught, the new regime offered only a dim reflection of the glory attained under the historic dynasties of Arpad, Anjou, and the Jagellons. Notwithstanding several conflicts which later arose between the Magyar political nation and the Habsburg and Habsburg-Lorraine dynasties, the ruling house still remained the supreme bond between all their lands, and particularly between their western and eastern parts. Yet, that allegiance was by no means of the same intensity in west and east.

There can be no question, the increasingly corroding effect of the internal conflict notwithstanding, that the armed forces with their unqualified obedience to the imperial and royal commander in chief constituted a strong consolidating factor. Nor is there any doubt either that by the eve of the First World War, the rise in general standards of higher education relative to the educational level attained by the permanent officers and long-term noncommissioned officers, as well as a definite social stagnation in the military organization itself, had adversely affected the prestige of the military. The deromanticized twentieth-century Austrian armed forces were not to the same extent as in bygone generations a supranational body with almost exclusive, highly respected characteristics of their own. Not to the detriment of their fighting qualities, but quite clearly to that of their consolidating influence, they had lost much of their splendid social and supranational isolation. They had become increasingly tied to the nationally particularly conscious lower-middle-class milieu from which most of the members of the officer class came and to which most of the noncommissioned officers strove to rise.

Concerning the factor of religious affiliation as a consolidating influence, the Roman Catholic church was the strongest, best organized, most widespread and most deeply penetrating spiritual force. Yet minorities, such as the regionally less homogeneous Protestant groups and the even more widely scattered Jews, must be listed as well. Neither of the latter, particularly in their German and Magyar affiliations, could be relatively as free of national ties as the Roman Catholic majority church. Yet both of them were relatively more independent of the currents of intense nationalism which increasingly penetrated the Slavonic Greek Orthodox churches.

Nationalist ecclesiastic influence was, however, relatively negligible, whereas the supranational liberal and later socialist ideas challenged by [sic] the very dynamics of Catholic strength, checked to some extent the universal church power. This point must be kept in mind in any attempt to evaluate the consolidating influence of the Catholic church in regard to the empire structure.

More controversial is the problem of evaluating the influence of the bureaucracy, and of the aristocracy. As to the former, its social potency, prior to the Maria-Theresian centralistic reforms was, relatively speaking, rather slight. During the Maria-Theresian era bureaucracy became unquestionably a consolidating factor to be reckoned with. Yet afterward the system of centralism directed by a linguistic and cultural, though by and large not nationalistic, Germanism met increasing opposition from various national groups and eventually became infected by nationalism itself. Thus bureaucracy changed from a unifying into a partly, though only partly, divisive force.

As to the aristocracy, the whole history of the Habsburg monarchy shows a distinct conflict between what may be called the territorial aristocracy in the historico-political entities; namely, those Habsburg lands of independent cultural-political tradition, on the one hand, and the high court nobility at the administrative center of the empire in Vienna on the other. This conflict centered largely upon the claims to autonomous rights by the historico-political entities. It may be considered a struggle for recognition of traditional patterns of nationalism. In that struggle the territorial aristocracies formed a conservative spearhead, while the centralistic court aristocracy rallied on the side of the fence in the imperial camp—a force not less conservative, but strictly opposed to autonomous federalist tendencies. The social conflicts of the later nineteenth and early twentieth century increasingly forced the high nobility—with the major exception of the

Magyar aristocracy—*nolens volens* to the imperial, centralistic side. At that very time, however, the aristocracy as a major carrier of political power had clearly begun to decline in influence. To put it succinctly, the centripetal influence of the aristocracy prior to the later nineteenth century, had been checked by the centrifugal trends in the same class. By the time that the centripetal factor had become stronger, the aristocracy had lost much of its social and political influence.

There seems to be a clear relationship between the influence of the aristocracy and that of ideological supranational party affiliation. Court nobility, and in later stages aristocracy in general, undoubtedly represented a supranational conservative ideology, albeit not in the sense of a political party. In view of the characteristic structure of the Habsburg monarchy the effectiveness of any supranational party movements across the empire must be considered as highly questionable. Historico-political autonomism and regional traditions, as well as considerable divergences in socioeconomic levels between various ethnic units, were just as much responsible for this state of affairs as was the artificial structure of the Compromise of 1867 and the existence of integral nationalism in its specific sense.

The bond between conservative forces has always been their similarity in socio-cultural character. Parliamentary organization, indeed parliamentarianism in general, was not among their preferences. The same view, of course, was not held by liberalism. Yet liberalism, in the sense of nineteenth-century Continental political philosophy, was intrinsically associated with nationalism, though only in its later metastases with that of any integral brand of nationalism. In any case, national elements in the liberal heritage after 1848 quite frequently set up mutually exclusive and conflicting group objectives, strong enough to impede and even to block possible liberal supranational cooperation. Party cooperation of ethnic groups on a Catholic ideological basis was hardly more successful. A chief source of failure clearly lay in the fact that intergroup solidarity of interests was adequately represented in the church itself. Socioeconomic ties outside that one supreme religious solidarity were not distinct enough to maintain an empirewide party system on religious foundations.

Nevertheless, while neither conservatism nor liberalism succeeded in establishing effective political cooperation between ethnic groups, they did not fail altogether in regard to issues of agricultural reform, education, church-state relations and judicial procedure, or in establishing common platforms of political thinking which by "diffusion" spread at least to a limited extent. After all, supranational group organization, indeed, the whole system of political organization itself, was regarded as only a means, and not even the primary means, to the ends of these systems of social philosophy.

Rather different in this respect was the viewpoint of socialism. To socialism—in German-Austrian terms, Social Democracy—intergroup cooperation across the whole empire represented the very essence of its political objective. Effective political party organization was conceived as the primordial means to that end. Did Social Democracy therefore do any better as a unifying factor than conservatism or liberalism?

In the Habsburg monarchy socialism in theory—though by no means generally in practice—was a movement which stretched beyond and across national issues. In view of its predominant Marxian pattern there, socialism in fact tended to reach not only across the national units within the monarchy but beyond the boundaries of the monarchy as well. The Marxian concept of class struggle, however, clearly stands in counter position to that of amalgamation and sense of community. As such it certainly could not be considered an integrating factor. Marxian social political doctrine was in theory definitely opposed to the integration of an empire such as the Habsburg monarchy. In fact, however, its political influence in the monarchy was very limited. Taking a short-range view it is, nevertheless, correct to say that socialism within the monarchy maintained a supranational program opposed to the idea of national separatism. Such was for instance the semifederalist empire reform plan of Karl Renner. Yet, seen in a far wider context, socialism in Austria would eventually have been confronted with the necessity of choosing either the theoretically supranational—in practice the faintly German centralistic—program of Renner or the international line. The latter, in the last years preceding the First World War and during the war, tended increasingly toward support of "national self-determination," a cautious circumlocution for outright separation. The outcome of the war took the choice out of the hands of the socialist movements in the monarchy. The internationalist trends became stronger, and, according to its leaders, socialism could not have kept its identity if it had dissociated itself from its theoretical antitradition raison d'étre. The role of socialism within the monarchy thus was far too complex and too controversial to enable one to list it outright among the centripetal forces.

The same complexity holds true of the issue of economic unity. Theoretically the monarchy provided a large free-trade area, an apparently ideal supplementation of eastern agricultural abundance and industrial scarcity with western industrial surplus production and needs for eastern food supplies.

In practice the Habsburg monarchy by no means represented the overall ideal geographical and economic unit, often emphasized in post–World War I political literature. It may suffice here to note first a few geographical facts. The Littoral and Dalmatia, which comprised the monarchy's relatively short coastal stretch, were separated from the bulk of the imperial territory by the Karst Mountains, a factor not counterbalanced by the acquisition of the hinterland of Bosnia-Herzegovina. Galicia and Bukovina were severed from the Hungarian lowlands by the Carpathians. The high plains of mountain-girded Bohemia were open by way of the Elbe River into northern Germany and the North Sea, and not into the Danube Valley. The Habsburg realm, due to the length of its main river system, was often referred to as the Danube Monarchy, but it should always be remembered that the Danube flows into the isolated inland Black Sea, all but cut off from the Mediterranean, the main artery of traffic between western and eastern Europe.

Agriculture and industry did not balance each other as completely as is frequently assumed. The significance of the former far outweighed the latter. The main centers of industry were situated in parts of the Bohemian-Moravian-Silesian and Alpine-German-Austrian territories. The standards of agricultural production—lower than comparable ones in France, Great Britain or Germany—did not create the desired markets for the products of the industries in the western part of the monarchy. Yet social-political conditions in the empire, due particularly to the influence of the great estate owners, foremost among which [sic] were the Magyar aristocracy, worked against reform of agricultural living conditions on which the welfare of the major part of the monarchy's population depended. Consequently, the advantages of the great imperial customs union of 1850, modified by the Compromise of 1867, were never fully developed and, under the last decades prior to the First World War, they were in some measure actually wiped out.

These conditions affected the whole peasant class, particularly underprivileged national groups in Hungary, but to a lesser extent also the agricultural population in the Cisleithanian part of the monarchy. At the same time the rising resentment of national groups was directed against the financial banking centers in Vienna for their seeming (rather than actual) exploitation of these groups. Strong disintegrating forces striving for economic independence came increasingly to the fore among the various nationalities. While their influence was greater in industry than in finance, a strong overall effect was evident.

Thus the economic unity of the Habsburg monarchy, while a point to be emphasized—actually and even potentially far superior to the economic order of the postwar world, was in fact still far from ideal. The integrating influence of the economic factors in the Habsburg monarchy must therefore be evaluated with great caution.

The evolution and preservation of the monarchy, however, throughout approximately four centuries after 1526 obviously belies any attempt to belittle the consolidating effect of the factors of tradition, dynasty, religious affiliations, armed forces, bureaucracy, aristocracy, ideological supranational party associations, and economic system, which have been reviewed here. The serious qualifications discussed with regard to some of these factors should be considered therefore not as disintegrating influences but rather as special factors which helped to give the Danube Monarchy that unique structure which differentiated it from the usual pattern of the Western centralized nation-state.

The consolidating forces discussed above served the empire in varying degrees while it lasted. When it disintegrated, they were either destroyed in the process, as were the crown and army; paralyzed in their consolidating effect, as were the churches, the bureaucracy and aristocracy; or they were diverted from their previous courses into new ones leading straight toward disintegration, as for example the one-time supranational party ideologies and the economic interests, which soon began to work for autonomy and autarchy.

The overall cause of these changes was the impact of the basic issue of diverse nationalisms under conditions of international political crises and eventually war. Aside from these specific unfavorable conditions the problem of conflicting nationalisms unquestionably helped to give the empire its specific complex political character. This factor in itself would not necessarily have meant a life expectancy inferior to that of other contemporary political units, had it not been for the impact of external political pressures. This impact was a diversified one. It included, among other factors, the ideological evolution of conflicting nationalisms in outside centers, in the case of the Habsburg empire, primarily Pan-Germanism, Italian irredentism and Pan-Slavism.

Contrary to widely held views, the issue of economic and social backwardness does not seem to be involved at this point. Questions of agricultural reform, of political democratization on the basis of general equal franchise, and of other social problems were not primary factors in the overall question of the empire's existence, although they were of first-rate importance within the individual national orbits and between national groups of unequal political rights and social standing. To be sure, dissatisfaction rising from such issues may have turned some people against the crown, yet, more often than not, the empire idea—though not necessarily imperial practice—was identified as agent and guarantor of a fairer social deal.

Erich Voegelin

THE EMPIRE: VICTIM OF ARRESTED DEVELOPMENT

A German by birth, Erich Voegelin (b. 1901) began his academic career in Vienna but was forced by political circumstance to continue that career in the United States, where he has taught at a number of universities. A political scientist and scholar with wide-ranging historical interests, he was interested in the Habsburg monarchy and the succession state in which he had lived, as problems of political evolution. In the following selection he sets forth his theory that Austrian constitutional developments followed a clearly defined cyclical pattern.

The constitutional theories of Baron von Eötvös and the experiences of 1848–1849 clarify for us a political situation which has the following characteristics:

From Erich Voegelin, *Der Autoritäre Staat: ein Versuch über das österreichische Staatsproblem* (Vienna, Julius Springer Verlag, 1936), pp. 82–86. Translated by permission of Springer Verlag.

1. The *ancien régime* is penetrated by the national idea; as a consequence, a whole series of political factors and related tendencies are in part newly created, in part activated by the struggle [which nationalism precipitates], and particularly

2. the monarch is compelled to assume the role of constitutional ruler of a state;

3. the peoples of the old empire are forced to take up the role of constituent elements of a political corpus, of a constitutional organism which is being formed from the [old] empire;

4. at the same time the numbers of ethnic groups, which under the impetus of nationalism are being converted into that many political nations, make the creation of a single people, the Austrian nation governed by the Austrian state, impossible;

5. as a consequence, the monarch is unable to fulfill unequivocally the role of constitutional ruler, because each of the political nations wants to have a direct relationship to him and to evade thereby regular constitutional procedures; his role as medieval dynast and master of many peoples is thus exaggerated by nationalism;

6. the whole political structure remains in a state of uncertainty, between an empire (ruler and subjects) and state (monarch and citizenry);

7. every attempt to advance liberal constitutional forms strengthens the power of nationalism and threatens the empire with dissolution; consequently every such attempt is followed by regressive moves, which attempt to prevent the impending dissolution by an authoritarian strengthening of the central government.

These essentials of the political situation remained unchanged until the fall of the monarchy, and the emotional character of Austrian politics had been so thoroughly dominated [by these factors] during the seven decades of its existence that they continued to exercise a powerful influence on the history of republican Austria after 1918. Thus a whole series of typical features can be found in the constitutional measures of the old and the new Austria. The essence of the empire was dependent on the political situation remaining forever in flux, and the consequence of that was that the Austrian constitutional innovations typically found their stimulus not from internal pressures but from blows from outside. Austrian constitutional history, therefore, clearly and meaningfully derives its form from the [external] stimuli which in each case brought about a political crisis within the country and in consequence a wave of constitutional reforms. The revolution in Paris was the stimulus to the constitutional schemes of 1848, which led via the Pillersdorf constitution,[1] the Kremsier draft, the constitution by command of March 1849 to the absolutist New Year's Patent of 1851. The monarchy's loss of prestige during the 1850s as a consequence of the policy followed in the Crimean War and the unsuccessful Italian War of 1859 led to the series of constitutions, which begins with the Patent of 5 March 1860 strengthening the Reichsrat, progresses by way of the October Diploma of 1860 and the February Patent of 1861, and ends with the suspension of the constitution in the year 1865. The crisis was, however, not over; it was, in fact, worsened by the defeat of 1866 and led finally to the December constitution of 1867. A series of minor electoral reforms follows, leading up to the electoral reform of 1907 sponsored by the Beck cabinet and introducing general, equal, secret, and direct suffrage. This reform is to be attributed to the effects of the Russian revolution of 1905. . . .

This general outline can be filled out by detailed characteristics, which are typical of Austrian constitutional development and in fact throughout the monarchy. Constitutions were characteristically provisional, mere drafts. At the beginning the Pillersdorf constitution almost immediately became nothing more than a provisional constitution, merely providing for a constituent assembly. . . . The Kremsier constitution was never put into operation. Of the decreed constitution of 1849 only its least characteristic feature, the Reichsrat, ever materialized. The Patent of 5 March 1860 was provisional, the October Diploma never went into effect. The February Patent of 1861 contained some lasting elements (especially local regulations), but the enlarged legislature, the central body, never met. The strongly federalistic constitution of 1867 was obliged to give up precisely those features, and in the reform of 1873 [essentially] a unitary state was once again introduced in the Austrian half of the empire. . . .

Thus Austria's constitutional acts are not clear-cut decisions bringing a struggle to an end with the resulting situation designed in accordance with the wishes of the victor, but rather a series of acts brought about in each case by a specific stimulus and proceeding through repetitive phases that wind up in closed units. Each of the

---

[1] Draft constitution of April 1848, which lost its significance, except as the basis for a constituent assembly, when the Pillersdorf cabinet lost its ability to mediate between monarch and mob.

series of drafts, provisional versions, suspended powers constitutes in toto in the realm of political action a curve which, starting from the base point of absolutism, moves out in a democratic direction, merely to return once again, sooner or later, to an absolutist or authoritarian structure. Most certainly the cycles do not duplicate themselves in every respect. Each of the later ones contains some elements taken over from the earlier, and since the political agent of the movement is the liberal and national democratic ideology, during the cycles the democratic element becomes steadily stronger, so that even the final, authoritarian phases can be disguised as democratic. Only the first cycle ends with an openly confessed authoritarianism, that of the New Year's Patent of 1851. . . .

Because Austrian constitutional history does not consist of single constitutional measures, each standing alone as a more or less binding commitment of political power, but rather of a series of acts, in which a fluctuating situation is once again stabilized, it is impossible to say without equivocation what kind of constitution Austria had at any given time. The statement that a state at a particular moment has a particular constitution is only meaningful if a decision has been made; when, on the contrary, the essence of the political situation lies in putting off decision in order to keep the structure intact, then the constitution can only be described through the forces operating on it. We must keep away from the letter of individual constitutions, which cause the empire to appear at one moment as absolute monarchy, at another as constitutional, at one point as federal state, at another as unitary state. . . . We must comprehend the enduring forces at work in the situation, which from time to time are converted in the assorted constitutions into juridical instruments. . . .

The extraordinary situation that a people does not develop a single political will, while concurrently the power of the democratic idea and the political activity of the people advance, resulted in the Austrian form of authoritarian state, which with each cycle of constitutionalism, each wave of democratic action, becomes easier to discern: the authoritarian form of government was the only one which, in the light of the existing power structure, could keep the state together; yet at the same time democracy was the only source of legitimacy. The state lacked within itself any of that self-evident authority which in the western European nation-states was the inheritance of the centralized absolute monarchies, of an earlier transformation of the populace into a political nation. Austria entered the era of political nations as an empire; its internal diffIculties derived almost entirely from its delayed development into a state or nation. . . .

Jacques Droz

THE EMPIRE: VICTIM OF A LOSS OF POLITICAL WILL

Jacques Droz has made himself one of the outstanding figures of the new generation of French scholars. Born in 1909 and for many years a member of the history faculty at Clermont-Ferrand, he has been professor of history at the University in Paris since 1962. A specialist in German history, especially that of the first half of the nineteenth century, he has shown a remarkable capacity to judge the developments of central Europe sympathetically though not uncritically, but above all with a sense of their place in the larger perspective of European history. The following selection, written in 1960, brings out clearly the new European attitude towards nationalism.

As a result of the crisis of 1866 central Europe found itself irremediably divided between two empires [Austrian and German] and there seemed no conceivable possibility of recreating a unity between them, of rejoining their territories [into one nation]. Moreover, up until the First World War, the idea of *Mitteleuropa* enjoyed a relative eclipse, or at least was engulfed in larger ambitions, such as that of the *Drang nach Osten* [drive to the east]. The ties between Germany and the Austrian Empire progressively loosened, since Berlin found itself more and more oriented towards global politics. It required the formidable impulse of the war and of the blockade to awaken once again the feeling of solidarity among the peoples of central Europe. For the time being, interest in the multinational state was concentrated in Austria-Hungary; and it was in Austria-Hungary that the conflict between the dissolving principle of nationality and the historic forces of resistance unrolled. The Dual Monarchy was the object of a series of reforms

From Jacques Droz, *L'Europe Centrale: Évolution historique de l'idée de "Mitteleuropa"* (Paris, 1960), pp. 153, 161–181, 204–205. Translated by permission of Editions Payot-Paris.

which, in one form or another, utilized and gave depth to the notion of federalism. In 1914 the existence of the multinational state in the Danube basin was no longer seriously in doubt, despite the violence of the struggles which took place there; but, among all shades of opinion, German as well as non-German, the conviction arose that the coexistence of nations demanded a profound transformation of institutions. . . .

Thanks to the indifference of the Germans towards *Mitteleuropa* [between 1866 and 1914], Austria had to seek out herself the solution to the problems posed by the multinational state. Face to face with a Germany which embodied, in absolute contrast to herself, the idea of the national state and which was touched by only the most secondary of nationality problems, the Dual Monarchy was caught up by grave difficulties arising from the exasperation of opposing groups [with one another] and the struggle of nationality with nationality.

It would be supremely unjust not to recognize what the Austrian statesmen attempted [in an effort] to resolve the problem of nationalities solely because their efforts were not crowned with success and the monarchy did not succeed in surmounting the test of the war of 1914. From a purely technical viewpoint the Austrian administration, which was, like Parliament in England, "the spinal column of the empire," rose to the grandeur of its task: Austria could pass for a model state whose peoples enjoyed a maximum of freedom compatible with the constitution. It was undeniable that of all nations—save perhaps Switzerland—Austria was the one in which the rights and the interests of the various nationalities were most generously represented. The formula, according to which the Habsburgs governed their subjects "with a judicious distribution of discontent," is certainly brilliant but does not in any way correspond to historical truth.

The dominant problem was that of dualism, that perilous and uncertain path upon which the government set forth in 1867 and from which it was extremely difficult to depart. Numerous observers were in effect agreed in admitting that from the day the emperor took the oath to the crown of Hungary, the scepter which ought to have protected all the peoples of his empire without favoritism escaped from him and fell into the hands of the Magyars. It is certainly difficult to say whether, in 1867, another solution would have been possible; but it is certain that the dualistic system, less as a result of the terms of it than as a consequence of the rigidity with which it was applied, brought about the dislocation of the state. It is, moreover, an error to believe that the Compromise of 1867 would have conferred on the Magyars and on the Germans a comparable power in the two parts of the monarchy; that which was true for the Magyars was never true for the Germans, who maintained their supremacy in the lands west of the Leitha with difficulty. It very soon became clear that if the authorities in Vienna wanted to escape from the tutelage of the Magyars, it would be necessary to come to an agreement with the Slav peoples, thus giving the state a truly federal organization, which would have assured Austria the support of the various nationalities and obliged Hungary to come to terms. By contrast, in maintaining their alliance with the Magyars who egoistically defended their national interests, the Germans condemned themselves to impotence, for without in the least conciliating the Magyars, they made of the Slav peoples declared enemies.

A number of Austrian statesmen took this view of the situation. The government believed at one point that it had found the solution in an agreement with the federalistically inclined Czech aristocracy: the cabinet presided over by Count Hohenwart, in which, however, the preponderant role was played by the academic Socialist Albert Schäffle . . . proposed, in 1871, recognizing the kingdom of Bohemia and reorganizing the monarchy on a trialistic basis. . . . The failure of this attempt was fateful for the future of the monarchy: everything which followed collided with aroused [national] passions. . . . After so many fruitless attempts, and faced with the extension of the nationality conflict, the government believed that with the establishment of universal suffrage it would be able, while satisfying the essential claims of the Slavs, to turn the parties' attention to more specifically economic and social problems: it required the energy of Baron Beck to surmount the opposition of the German parties and to impose on Cisleithania a reform, in January of 1907, which entirely modified the equilibrium of the Reichsrat for the benefit of the Slavs, on the one hand, for that of the democratic parties (the Christian Socialists and the Socialists), on the other. But the attempt did not succeed; the crisis which the annexation of Bosnia-Herzegovina (1908) called forth reawakened national passions in all their virulence. The successors of Baron Beck were driven to abandon all attempts at reform and followed a policy of governing from day to day.

How does one explain the failure of these different attempts at reform? It has been justly asserted that it was Hungary, anxious to evict the government in Vienna wholly from its affairs and to maintain its uncontested hegemony over the nationalities subject to it, which bears the responsibility for this state of affairs. Betraying the promises of liberalism which were contained in the [Hungarian] Nationality Law of 1868, the Magyars never ceased, up to 1914, pursuing a policy of assimilating the elites of the nationalities [in Hungary] and thus systematically opposing all efforts directed toward a trialistic or federalistic organization of the Dual Monarchy. The government of Francis Joseph gave way to Hungarian pretensions because it did not believe it possible to renege on the promises made at the time of the coronation [in Hungary, in 1867]: Austrian statesmen were thus forbidden to work out to its conclusion any political idea, because any idea of that nature could not fail, sooner or later, to collide with the reactions in Hungary and because the latter had to remain, legally, outside the discussion. By scrupulously respecting the clauses of dualism, they were condemned to see escaping from them one after another all their reforming attempts. The Hungarian opposition thus constituted an element of explanation.

But it is still necessary to provide the reasons which led the government in Vienna to preserve vis-à-vis the Magyars this passive and discouraging formalism. To tell the truth—and this is without doubt the most plausible interpretation of the final resignation of the government—Vienna increasingly felt that the nationalities question in Austria-Hungary was an international question, linked to the reactions of the various imperial powers, dependent on the ambitions of the Great Powers. Italian irredentism? South-Slav nationalism? Sympathy of the Czech nation for Russia? So many problems which were not soluble within the framework of the monarchy and on which international rivalries weighed. If Francis Joseph hesitated to overturn the status quo for the benefit of a federalistic solution, it was because he had the decided feeling that federalism would not protect the diverse elements of his empire from the covetousness of his neighbors, that it would, on the contrary, encourage them. He therefore resigned himself, on grounds of state necessity, to immobility. . . .

Austrian liberalism, that political faith which was always a powerful influence among the bureaucracy and which was largely German in character and centralistic in tendency, but which also found an echo in business circles and certain intellectual groups, suffered growing discredit even among those elements most deeply attached to the existing political and social order. A certain number of political writers of conservative hue believed, in effect, that nationalism could only be effectively combated in an Austria converted wholly into a federal state where the various ethnic groups had already received autonomy. They thought that the claims of the subject nations should not be rejected and that "Greater Austria" should become a common homeland for all those whom fate had obliged to live under the same roof. Hostile to all forms of centralism, they pushed the consequences of their ideas to the point of combating dualism, whose disappearance was certainly the precondition of all political regeneration. . . .

One must take note of the publication of the book by Aurel Popovici, *The United States of Greater Austria* (1906), which was a manifesto of the Greater Austria movement. A Rumanian from Transylvania, Popovici had been a victim of Magyar nationalism, and he hoped for protection against Hungary in an Austria regenerated by federalism. The book, in fact, uses the suggestions of quite a number of writers who sought to redirect, in this sense, the political life of the Dual Monarchy: the French publicist Saint-René Taillandier, the Belgian Émile de Lavelaye, the [French] historian Louis Eisenmann, whose celebrated thesis on *The Austro-Hungarian Compromise* (1904) had just appeared, the Austrian R[ichard] Charmatz, who had demonstrated the difficuties a federalistic organization would encounter in Hungary and suggested that Cisleithania alone should be given a government of national autonomy, while Transleithania should remain under a territorial system, the sole bond between the two states being reduced to a personal union [through the monarch].

In response to these authors, Popovici tried to demonstrate that in the reconstruction of Austria-Hungary one did not have to take into account the little national enclaves, which were in any case destined to disappear through assimilation or transfer of the population, and that in consequence it was only necessary to consider the large national groups; according to him, one could not have national autonomy without national territory. But he did not wish to see these territories delimited according to the ancient historic-political entities, "survivals of the Middle Ages," but rather in conformance with ethnic and linguistic actuality. Inspired by the program of Kremsier [where an elected Assembly had devised a federalistic constitution for Austria in 1849], he thought he could distinguish fifteen national groups [in Austria]: German Austria, German Bohemia, German Moravia, Czech

Bohemia, Polish Galicia, Ruthenian Galicia, Rumanian Transylvania, Croatia, Carniola and the Slovene country, Slovakia, Serbian Voivodina, the Magyar territories of Hungary, the Szekler country, the Italian Trentino, Trieste and the Italian sections of Istria; he foresaw also national autonomy for the Jews extended over the whole of the Dual Monarchy. These fifteen territories should enjoy autonomous institutions, and their governors, designated by the emperor, would be responsible to national legislatures; each would use its own tongue as the official language, and those imperial officials designated to keep an eye on the administration would also be required to know it. Popovici was convinced that "all the peoples of the Danube basin are entirely dedicated to the Austrian idea, for an undeniable community of interests exists among them." The Dual Monarchy was "a big, old house" which had suffered from family quarrels, but it could be made habitable "by dividing it into apartments." He would keep in his project, however, some federal institutions with extensive powers: legislative power in the hands of two houses, one elected by universal suffrage, the other formed from persons of prominence; the executive power [would be] constituted by a forty-two member council designated by the national legislatures and presided over by an imperial chancellor. German would remain the imperial language and would have to be spoken by all functionaries.

The interest in Popovici's program rested on the hearing which he had acquired in the entourage of Archduke Francis Ferdinand. As vague and changeable, so it seemed to him, as the political thought of the heir to the Habsburg throne might be, he certainly had in common with Popovici a distaste for Magyar centralism and the desire to break the rebellious spirit of the Magyars for the benefit of the nationalities groaning under their yoke. "In his conversations," wrote his confidant Edmund Steinacker, "I recall particularly the assertion that he had no antipathy to any of the peoples of the monarchy, and that he measured his affection [for them] by the extent of the economic and military sacrifices they were prepared to make to the collective interest; but of the Magyar oligarchy and its political leaders he would not hear a word. He considered the reform of the dualistic constitution as necessary, and he had already decided to operate on it, gently and with respect for legal forms, if possible, but with the violence of blood and iron, if necessary."

From this newly developed hostility towards the Magyars sprang the support he never failed to give to the claims of the Croats, though it did not make him a systematic Slavophile: he never had any sympathy for the Czechs or the Poles. "Say to your Croatians," he wrote to Count Bombelles in 1909, "that they should hang onto their traditional loyalty: as soon as I am on the throne I will make good all the injustice of which they have been the victims." Francis Ferdinand loved to repeat that it was the Croats under Jellačič who had saved the government in 1848, and he appreciated the depth of their Catholic faith. In the movement of "Pan-Croatism" he saw a means not merely of weakening Hungary but of cutting the ground from under the feet of the Serbs, a preoccupation which was linked to his views on the foreign policy of the monarchy. In any case, one finds this tendency to favor the Croats in all the successive projects the heir to the throne worked out for the reorganization of the monarchy: whether they consisted of a federal statute for the estates of the crown; or whether they envisaged—as was the case between 1903 and 1909—a trialistic system of Austria, Hungary, and the South Slavs; or whether, disturbed by the developing spirit of the Serbs, he came back to the program of Popovici for ethnic federalism or even a simple dualism with a special statute for Bosnia-Herzegovina. . . .

Undeniably, the political thought of Francis Ferdinand was conservative and authoritarian: it was for him first and foremost a question of reinforcing the power of the crown and of restoring the empire to its ancient splendor. "Among the means [available] to unify the people," he said to the archbishop of Breslau, "I number the dynasty, the Catholic religion, and the German language as instruments of culture." At bottom he shared the aristocratic views current in his day, especially among the Bohemian and German aristocracy, and the introduction of universal suffrage into Cisleithania was repugnant to him. Above all he rejected any and all measures that could weaken the army or reduce its capability of acting. But he was perfectly well aware of the dangers that linguistic quarrels could mean for Austria; and he thought an increase in the prerogatives of the crown was not inconsistent with territorial autonomy for nationalities equal among themselves. The education which his tutor, the "great German" historian Onno Klopp had given him, his travels to the United States, his own political experience: all these led him to federalism, which by destroying the Magyar hegemony would, he hoped, increase the central power.

Thus the program of a supranational, federative, and Catholic Austria was born among those whom it is convenient to call "the Belvedere group" [from the palace occupied by Francis Ferdinand], which drew in those ambitious men who, together with some faithful friends, hoped to gain control by the accession of a new monarch. One encounters among them numerous political figures belonging to the opposition or to the subject nationalities: the Hungarian Liberal J. Kristóffy; Edmund Steinacker, chief of the Germans in Hungary; the Rumanians Popovici, Vaida-Voivod, and Miron Cristea; the Slovakian M. Hodža; the Croat J. Frank. The Austrians [among them] belonged to the [business] world or to the press—F. Funder, editor-in-chief of the Catholic *Reichspost* [Imperial Post]; L. v. Chlumecky, editor of the *Oesterreichische Rundschau* [Austrian Survey]; the publicist Th[eodor] v. Sosnosky; F. Danzer, proprietor of the *Armeezeitung* [Army News]—or to the army, like the chief of the general staff, General Conrad von Hötzendorf, who shared the ideas of the archduke on many points, except for those on war, which he believed inevitable and hoped [to make it a] preventive [war]—or to finance, like the director of the *Kredit-Anstalt,* A. v. Spitzmüller. One encountered finally members of the aristocracy, like Count Clam-Martinic, advisor to the archduke on domestic matters, and O. Czernin, future minister of foreign affairs of the Dual Monarchy, whose diverse memoranda addressed at that time to Belvedere pushed Francis Ferdinand toward a "Caesarian" policy beginning with the introduction by decree of universal suffrage in Hungary. In view of this motley entourage, a certain confusion which characterized the activities of the prince is scarcely surprising. Nonetheless, Francis Ferdinand was without doubt the sole representative of the dynasty who could [have] cope[d] with the nationality problem: all the hopes of those who believed in the future of the state rested on him. His deeply religious sense of obligation constituted a guarantee of his sincerity and of the seriousness with which he would apply his ideas. The hostility which the liberal middle class of Austria never ceased to exhibit toward him is sufficient proof that he clearly saw the evils from which his country suffered. . . .

What were they, then, the forces of resistance to the dissolving action of nationalities on the eve of the First World War?

The conviction remains profound and general that, in all the organization projects which we have just reviewed, that secular community which constituted the Austrian monarchy was necessary, not only to the peoples who inhabited it, but for the good of Europe. The reproach later directed toward Austria, of being a "prison of peoples," of having "vassalized nations," had not yet made its appearance, and we are well aware that the destruction of the supranational monarchy, which in the last analysis had given to the nationalities [of that region] a durable peace and an equitable justice, signified with but a brief reprieve chaos and anarchy. One hoped for a generation of institutions within the framework of the existing frontiers, especially as the nationalities still felt that they were united one to another by common interests and common memories.

However, in the face of the failure of the various reform efforts and the persistence of "muddling through," an enormous lassitude seized the spirits of even the better men. What the monarchy suffered from, as Kurt Schuschnigg later confirmed, was "lack of will": the statesmen were "tired of monarchy." The *opinio necessitatis,* the force of necessity, which had been a powerful argument for the partisans of the system and which [at the same time] had kept the malcontents on the road to rebellion, had lost in many eyes its magic significance. Most seriously, the affairs of Austria had begun to elude Austrian control, and it is that which convinces one, in the light of the international tension [of those years] and of the appetites of neighboring powers, that a satisfactory solution was no longer possible within the existing European framework.

Stephen Borsody

THE EMPIRE: AN UNREALIZED FEDERAL UNION

Stephen Borsody, a native Hungarian, graduate of Charles University in Prague, former editor and diplomat, has used his intimate personal knowledge of the Danube Basin to enrich his studies of that area. Profoundly impressed by the tragic consequences of political weakness vis-à-vis stronger neighbors, Borsody detailed the results in his Triumph of Tyranny *(New York, 1960). The following selection is from a paper written for the Comparative Communism Program of the University Center for International Studies of the University of Pittsburgh in 1968.*

The break-up of this Dual Monarchy of many more than two nations is better known as dissolution or dismemberment—two terms loaded with controversy, expressing two extreme poles of interpretation. Break-up is preferable not only because it creates no controversy. Its advantage primarily is that it encompasses both what is meant by dismemberment (the rather rash way the territory of Austria-Hungary was carved up into nation-states) and by dissolution (the long process of disintegration which led to the catastrophe of 1918). Irrespective of terminology, the break-up of the Danubian empire of 50 million people and eleven nations—either full grown or on the way to political maturity—is one of the most significant events of the twentieth century. As a problem of historical interpretation, the event remains on the controversial list. However, if viewed in broader perspective, this fascinating drama of contemporary history may very well impress the interpreter (pondering Europe's fate from the vantage point of 1968) essentially as a clash between nationalism and federalism —nationalism playing the role of the undesirable but successful suitor of Danubia, while federalism that of the desirable but rejected one.

The conflict between nationalism and federalism in the Danube region goes, of course, well beyond the events of fifty years ago. Ever since the struggle between the modern forces of nationalism and the old Habsburg order began, federalism represented the program of sensible compromise—and as such the hope of those who were in

From Stephen Borsody, "The Break-up of Austria–Hungary: Fifty Years After" (Reprint No. 1, Comparative Communism Program, University Center for International Studies, University of Pittsburgh, Pittsburgh, 1968), pp. 1–5, 7. Reprinted by permission of the author.

search of a "solution" capable of rebuilding the empire on modern foundations. With the triumph of German nationalism under Bismarck in 1866 and 1870, the federative solution of the Habsburg problem became more desirable than ever, but in practice it also became less likely than before. In 1867, the Habsburg compromise with the rising tide of nationalism took the form of the Austro-Hungarian Compromise, which was not a federative reform. On the contrary, the dualist system dividing the power in the empire between Magyars and Germans blocked the road to the broader compromise which federalization of the empire required.

*   *   *

The break-up of defeated Austria-Hungary in 1918 was a triumph for those nationalities, mostly Slavs, who [were] oppressed under the dualist system. The simultaneous Bolshevik revolution in neighboring Russia added revolutionary stimulus to the explosive situation in central Europe. But neither the Russian revolution, nor the sufferings of economic exploitation under Austro-Hungarian class rule, nor the social disintegration caused by war, had as decisive an impact on the course of events in 1918–1919 as did the explosion of pent-up forces of nationalism. The collapse of Austria-Hungary and the rise of the new order constituted first and foremost a nationalist revolution. Furthermore, the aspirations of this revolution expressed themselves primarily in territorial demands. Not freedom under democracy (the great slogan of the victorious Allies in the First World War) but territory was the prime interest of the nations of the Danube region in their moment of gaining independence. Democracy was the slogan that endeared the cause of the oppressed nationalities to the liberal West; but territory was the prize for which the liberated had fought, in a frenzy of nationalism, with all their available means of force and propaganda.

Yet, strangely enough, while so much that is undesirable in nationalism was triumphant, both those leaving and entering the scene of central European history were invoking the highly desirable ideas of federalism. The exit of the last Habsburg, Emperor Charles, was accompanied by the tunes of federalism perfunctorily aiming at saving the empire that no more existed. His manifesto of 16 October 1918 proclaimed that "Austria shall, as its people desire, become a

Federal State." True, Hungary's ruling classes remained irreconcilable foes of federalism to the very end; the Budapest government threatened to cut off food supplies to Austria if Emperor Charles included Hungary in his federalization plans, which explains why the imperial manifesto explicitly excluded the lands of the Hungarian crown from the monarchy's federative reconstruction. On the other hand, after the collapse of the monarchy, historic Hungary's federalization became the program of the Magyar revolutionary republic headed by the pro-Entente liberal aristocrat, Count Mihály Károlyi. And, whereas Emperor Charles's appeal to federalism was an empty gesture, Count Károlyi's program was a sincere move seeking reconciliation among the Danubian people under the banner of democracy and the Wilsonian principle of national self-determination. It was the great tragedy of 1918 that the Magyar democrats did not participate with the liberated nationalities in building a new order, for they were eminently suitable partners for a sensible compromise. The late Oscar Jászi, a member of Károlyi's revolutionary cabinet and chief spokesman of reconciliation among the nationalities, ranks to this day as one of the most outstanding advocates of Danubian federalism.

The program that carried the day when Austria-Hungary collapsed was the liberation plan of the Western Allies. "National self-determination"—the lofty principle of that plan, associated with President Wilson's name—unfortunately turned into a policy of territorial punishment and territorial reward. An irreconcilable conflict existed between the territorial demands, supported by the victorious Allies, and the Wilsonian principle of national self-determination. Only a federal reconstruction of the Danube region could resolve the conflict—and the experts knew it. The American Peace Commission's committee in charge of boundary questions clearly recognized this fact when it reported to Wilson that it was unable to discover a territorial division of Austria-Hungary which would be both just and practical. The committee's report pointed out that the difficulties could be solved only if the boundaries were to be drawn "with the purpose of separating not independent nations but component portions of a federalized state."

The leaders of the liberated denounced the idea of a continued Danubian union as contrary to the interests of peace and democracy. Preservation of a Danubian empire in any shape or form, they argued, would serve no other purpose but abetting German and Magyar imperialism. Yet, while opposed to a broader Danubian federation, they appealed to the federative principle as a means of achieving their self-centered nation-state objectives. The Corfu Declaration of July 1917, proclaiming the union of the South Slavs under the rule of the Serbian dynasty, anticipated the foundation of the Yugoslav Kingdom as a federal state. The Pittsburgh Agreement of May 1918, signed between T. G. Masaryk and Americans of Slovak descent, stipulated autonomy for the Slovaks in Czechoslovakia. Similarly, the spokesmen for the Ruthenes, at a congress at Scranton, Pennsylvania, in December 1918, agreed to join Czechoslovakia on a federal basis. The Rumanians of Transylvania, at their meeting at Alba Julia in November 1918, proclaimed unity with the Kingdom of Rumania with the assurances of autonomy. And Bessarabia, too, upon leaving the Russian Empire in April 1918, proclaimed unity with Rumania on terms of autonomy.

Expectations among the weaker victors for a federal tie with their stronger partners were no more fulfilled than were the hopes of the vanquished for a fair execution of the Wilsonian principle of national self-determination. New struggles for and against national priorities and privileges began immediately following the collapse of Austro-Hungarian hegemony. The nationalist revolution of 1918–1919 broke up the Danubian empire of the Habsburgs; it also shattered the chances of federal union among the Danubian people.

*   *   *

The Czech democrats were the most articulate defenders of the nation-state order, while Magyar conservatives (restored to power under Admiral Horthy's counterrevolution) excelled in extolling historic supranationalism in the postwar era—a division of labor which raised the prestige of the postwar settlement, but was of no help to the cause of federalism. . . .

No partisan of freedom and democracy could rebuke Masaryk for his dislike of Austria-Hungary. Justifiable, too, was his view that the Dual Monarchy would never [have] be[en] capable of carrying out the necessary reforms—a conclusion, incidently, which Masaryk, a one-time believer in the monarchy's federalization, had reached well before launching his wartime anti-Habsburg campaign. But the plans thus born in his mind which, in turn, became the program of the Allies for the reorganization of central Europe, were fed by resentment rather than foresight. As the Czech historian Otakar Odložilik put it: "Masaryk saw the principal enemy in the past." Or, as the Austrian-born Hans Kohn said of Masaryk's policy: "In the hour of triumph, it was overlooked that victory was due to an unusual combination of circumstances which might not last." . . . Masaryk himself, one of the principal founders of the new nationalist order—did not believe that the nation-state was an end in itself. When in 1918 he returned from exile as president of freshly founded Czechoslovakia he said to his friends: "We destroyed Austria, but now we must somehow devise a way to put her together again." He was hopeful that the liberated nations would eventually organize themselves into greater units. However, he considered this the task of the next generation. "The Danubian people, in order to unite, must first be free," he said. It is a pity he did not supply the Allies with a liberation policy founded on the premise that the Danubian people could not be free unless they were united.

An Allied federalist liberation policy, emphasizing the democratic solidarity of the Danubian people, could have perhaps united victors and vanquished. In that case, T. G. Masaryk, Edvard Beneš, Karl Renner, Otto Bauer, Mihály Károlyi, Oscar Jászi, Milan Hodža, and other liberal Danubians—essentially all of them of the same democratic persuasion—might have joined forces as founders of a Danubian federation, instead of going their separate national ways. In concrete political terms, a federalist liberation policy would have meant a program of preserving the unity of the Habsburg Empire without the Habsburgs. This "third road"—going beyond the much discussed alternatives of partitioning or preserving the Habsburg realm—has never been tried out; it cannot be known whether it had a chance to succeed as an objective of Allied policy in 1918–1919. In view of the now world-wide triumph of nationalism it may appear that the substitution of the Habsburg Empire with nation-states was the course that history had to take in central Europe, too. On the other hand, in few places of the world was there a greater need than in central Europe for a structure of government different from that of the centralized Western nation-state. The West Europeans themselves, as founders of a movement for a supranational Europe, after the Second World War took the initiative toward reversing the nationalist trend. In the Danube region such an initiative was badly needed already after the First World War.

. . . Freedom and independence, which the break-up of Austria-Hungary was believed to deliver to the Danubian people fifty years ago, is still an unfulfilled promise. If these precious rights can survive at all in that part of Europe, most likely a broader federal political structure could best create and safeguard them. Whether it would take one or more regional, or an all-embracing Continental or world federation to achieve these goals, is a matter of speculation. At any rate, the conflict between nationalism and federalism is still the main, if not necessarily the most visible, internal issue in the Danube region.

Suggestions for Additional Reading

The reader who wants to explore the problems of the Austrian Empire more deeply will find only scattered material in English. True, the fate of eastern Europe after World War II led many people to think again about the Danube Valley. No longer did the settlement decreed by the victorious Allies in 1919 appear to be the self-evident and logical solution to an historic problem. But the number of scholars and specialists writing on this problem in English, in part perhaps because of the linguistic hurdles to be overcome, is still very small. Yet further investigation repays itself, and some very good works have appeared; hopefully their number will increase steadily.

The era since World War II has produced three very good general histories of the Austrian Empire in the period 1848–1914. The first to appear is Robert A. Kann's *The Multinational Empire* (New York, 1950), a monumental study of nationalism and the efforts to solve the problems it raised within the empire. *The Habsburg Monarchy, 1867–1914* (Cambridge, Mass., 1951) by the late Arthur J. May, though comprehensive in its presentation of information, sometimes suffers from a textbook style and a lack of insight into motives. The Englishman C. A. Macartney enjoys the advantage of intimate personal knowledge of many parts of the empire. His *The Habsburg Empire, 1790–1918* (London, 1968) is not without occasional opinionated judgments, but the last half of the book offers a sympathetic yet critical treatment of the empire between 1848 and 1918. In addition, Victor L. Tapié's *Monarchie et peuples du Danube* (Paris, 1969; English translation by Stephen Hardman, London, 1971), while covering the whole imperial history from 1526 onwards, contains both an astonishing amount of information, especially on economic and social developments, and a detached and judicious evaluation.

Far less profound treatments of the development of the monarchy will be found in A. J. P. Taylor's *The Habsburg Monarchy, 1809–1918* (London, 1948) and Adam Wandruszka's *The House of Habsburg* (Garden City, 1964), both of which were intended to appeal to the general reader. Erich Zöllner's *Geschichte Österreichs* (Munich, 1963), a sound and balanced survey, has not as yet been translated into English, but for those who want a quick overview of Austrian foreign policy there is Barbara Jelavich's *The Habsburg Empire in European Affairs, 1814–1918* (Chicago, 1969).

Those who wish to view the empire through the eyes of earlier generations should turn first to Henry Wickham Steed, correspondent of the London *Times* in Vienna prior to the First World War and later editor of that distinguished paper. Steed wrote what was really for many years the only available overall description in English of the Habsburg monarchy (first edition, London, 1913). Though well informed as to the structure of the monarchy, Steed's basic approach is journalistic; and the work is characterized by an unacceptable quantity of anticlerical and anti-Semitic prejudice. Yet Steed's book was widely read when it appeared. Along with the works of R. W. Seton-Watson, who became a kind of international spokesman for the various Slavic nationalities—*Racial Problems in Hungary* (London, 1908); *The Southern Slav Question and the Habsburg Monarchy* (London, 1911); *Absolutism in Croatia* (London, 1912)—Steed's book is responsible for the lack of sympathy towards the empire in English governing circles of those days.

The interwar period is rather devoid of useful treatments of the problem of the empire, largely because most people in the West tended to view the settlement of 1918 as the consummation of natural, and inevitable, historical processes. For the residents of the former empire, the shock of dissolution appeared to have stilled most voices. The two major works which appeared were Viktor Bibl's *Der Zerfall Österreichs* (2 vols., Vienna, 1922–1924) and Oskar Jászi's *The Dissolution of the Habsburg Monarchy* (Chicago, 1929). These two books carry basically the same message: the empire was already moribund in the late nineteenth century because the ruling classes failed to democratize the empire's governing institutions. Good will was all on the side of the popular representatives, their opponents were characterized at best by lethargy, at worst by evil intent. The two works complement one another nicely, Jászi having been a Hungarian liberal, Bibl an Austrian.

It is gratifying to see the way in which first the Austrians themselves, and subsequently historians of other lands, have awakened from the trauma which the collapse of the empire initially provoked. This awakening has been particularly valuable in stimulating more detailed and dispassionate investigation of the segments of Austrian development between 1848 and 1914. For the reader who wants to explore the personality of the emperor in greater depth there is, however, little that is new. The letters exchanged between Francis Joseph and his actress confidante, Frau Schratt can be found in J. Bourgoing, *Briefe Kaiser Franz Josefs und Frau K.S.* (Vienna, 1949). They have now been translated into English (Albany, N.Y., 1968) and offer some insight into the personality of the emperor but little into his governing philosophy. The imperial family has attracted some popular attention, for instance in the journalistic biographies *Elizabeth, Empress of Austria* by Egon Corti (New Haven, 1936) and Richard Barkeley, *The Road to Mayerling,* (London, 1959), a biography of Crown Prince Rudolf, but these emphasize the personal rather than the political element and provide little help in interpreting the constitutional role of the emperor.

More valuable is A. Schwarzenberg's biography *Prince Felix zu Schwarzenberg, Prime Minister of Austria, 1848–1852* (New York, 1947), which, despite the author's understandable admiration for a distinguished scion of his house, is not without insight into the historical problems created by Schwarzenberg's policy. Rudolf Kiszling's *Fürst Felix zu Schwarzenberg* (Graz-Köln, 1951) does not differ very much in interpretation but makes use of official archives. Stadion has yet to receive the biography he deserves, but the concept of *Mitteleuropa* which underlay Bruck's work is covered in the introductory sections of H. C. Meyer, *Mitteleuropa in German Thought and Action, 1815–1945* (The Hague, 1955).

None of the great figures of constitutional experimentation have received biographical treatment except Count Andrássy and, of course, the emperor himself. Redlich's exhaustive treatment of this problem is still the best, but there are so many details in his *Staats- und Reichsproblem* that the overall picture is difficult to extract. A discussion of Schmerling's efforts is to be had in F. Fellner, *Das Februarpatent von 1861* (Vienna, 1959). New consideration of the Compromise itself is found in two books of collected essays by various specialists: *Der österreichischungarische Ausgleich von 1867: Vorgeschichte und Wirkungen* (ed. *Forschungsinstitut für den Donauraum,* Vienna, 1967) and *Der österreichischungarische Ausgleich von 1867: seine Grundlagen und Auswirkungen* (Munich, *Buchreihe der sudostdeutschen historischen Kommission,* vol. 20, Munich, 1968).

The political consequences of the Ausgleich as seen in their effects on various parts of the empire are examined in the classic by Louis Eisenmann, *Le Compromis Austro-Hongrois de 1867: Etude sur le dualisme* (Paris, 1904); the books of William A. Jenks, *Austria under the Iron Ring* (Charlottesville, 1965) and *The Austrian Electoral Reform of 1907* (New York, 1950); and particularly the 1967 issue, volume three, of the *Austrian History Yearbook,* papers by an assortment of specialists on the Austrian Empire dealing with "The Nationality Problem in the Habsburg Monarchy in the Nineteenth Century: A Critical Appraisal." Elisabeth Wiskemann devotes the opening chapters of *Czechs and Germans* (London, 1938) to the latter part of the nineteenth century. An interesting Marxian interpretation of the nationality problem in the Habsburg Empire will be found in Péter Hanák, ed., *Die nationale Frage in der österreichisch-ungarischen Monarchie, 1900–1918* (Budapest, 1966), a collection of papers by various eastern European scholars first presented at a conference in Budapest in May, 1964.

The last stages of the empire seem to have attracted rather more interest than its earlier phases, especially recently. Arthur J. May capped a scholarly career dedicated to study the Austrian Empire with a monumental two-volume account of its last years, *The Passing of the Hapsburg Monarchy* (Philadelphia, 1966). Shorter, but still worth reading, is Z. A. B. Zeman's *The Break-up of the Habsburg Empire* (London, 1914–1918). In 1968 the Österreichisches Ost- und Südosteuropa Institut organized an international meeting in Vienna to discuss the dissolution of the empire. The papers presented at that meeting have now been published as *Die Auflösung des Habsburgerreiches* (Munich, 1970).

Material dealing with the economic development of the Habsburg monarchy is scant. Hans Meier's *100 Jahre österreichische Wirtschaftsentwicklung, 1848–1948* (Vienna, 1949) covers much the same ground as Heinrich Benedikt's book. A limited amount of largely statistical information is contained in Frederick Hertz, *The Economic Problems of the Danubian States* (London, 1947), the first chapter of which deals with the period before 1918. Hans Rosenberg introduced his ideas regarding the effects of the Great Depression in his article "Political and Social Consequences of the Great Depression in Central Europe, 1873–1896" in the *Economic History Review,* 1st ser., vol. 12. Two special studies are: F. Sugar, *The Industrialization of Bosnia-Herzegovina* (Seattle, 1963) and Karl F. Helleiner, *The Imperial Loans: a Study in Financial and Diplomatic History* (Oxford, 1965).

A comprehensive and sympathetic treatment of the rise of the Social Democratic movement in Austria and its effect on the problem of political loyalty is given in Hans Mommsen, *Die Sozialdemokratie und die Nationalitätenfrage im habsburgischen Vielvölkerstaat* (Vienna, 1963). A classic statement of the left-wing Social Democratic position is Otto Bauer's *Die Nationalitätenfrage und die Sozialdemokratie* (Vienna, 1907). The opening chapters of C. A. Macartney's *The Social Revolution in Austria* (Cambridge, 1926) offer a rather didactic treatment of the Austrian Social Democratic movement in the pre–World War I years.

The problem of the multinational state in an abstract sense is treated with much insight in Macartney's *National States and National Minorities* (London, 1934). Erich Zöllner surveys historically the changing concept of Austria in his article, "Formen und Wandlungen des Österreichbegriffes," in *Historica,* edited by Hugo Hantsch, Erich Voegelin, and Franco Valsecchi (Vienna, 1965). Srbik does much the same thing, but with more bibliographical information, in "Österreichs Schicksal im Spiegel des geflügelten Wortes," an essay which appears with others by him in *Aus Österreichs Vergangenheit* (Salzburg, 1949). A general history of federalism in central Europe, though focusing primarily on its application to Germany, is Ernst Deuerlein's *Föderalismus: die historischen und philosophischen Grundlagen des föderativen Prinzips* (Munich, 1972). Some rather sophisticated theorizing about the concept of the nation and its use and misuse by governments can be found in four articles by two leading German historians, Hans Rothfels and Theodor Schieder. Rothfels brought out "Grundsätzliches zum Problem der Nationalität," in the *Historische Zeitschrift,* vol. 174 (1952) and "Die Nationsidee in westlicher und östlicher Sicht," in *Osteuropa und der deutsche Osten,* Ser. I, Book 3 (1956). The two articles by Schieder are "Idee und Gestalt des übernationalen Staates seit dem 19. Jahrhundert," in *Historische Zeitschrift,* vol. 184, 1957, and "Nationalstaat und Nationalitätenproblem," in *Zeitschrift für Ostforschung,* vol. 1, 1952.

For those who want to examine the consequences of the collapse of the monarchy for the peoples of eastern Europe, Stephen Borsody has written *The Triumph of Tyranny: the Nazi and Soviet Conquest of Central Europe* (London and New York, 1960).

THE PROBLEMS IN EUROPEAN CIVILIZATION SERIES
(Arranged in approximate chronological order)

(continued from inside front cover)